49 Business Ideas
to Make Money in (Legal) Marijuana

49 Business Ideas to Make Money in (Legal) Marijuana

Copyright © Northstar Ink, January 2015

Disclaimer   Although the author and publisher have made every effort to ensure that the information in this book was correct at press time, the author and publisher do not assume and hereby disclaim any liability to any party for any loss, damage, or disruption caused by errors or omissions, whether such errors or omissions result from negligence, accident, or any other cause. While the author has made every effort to provide accurate phone, online & other contact info at this time of publication, neither the publisher nor the author can assume any responsibility for errors, or changes that occur after publication. Further, we have no control over and can't be responsible for any third-party web site's contents.

This book is not intended as a substitute for legal advice from a licensed attorney in your state. The reader should consult a lawyer knowledgeable in the subject matter of this book to get specific advice and counsel.

The information in this book is meant to supplement, not replace, such legal advice. Like any business opportunity, there are certain inherent risks in using the ideas in this guide. The authors and publisher advise readers to take full responsibility for their compliance with local state and federal regulations, and understand the risks.

Getting Started in Legal Marijuana

GOOD NEWS: THERE IS VIRTUALLY no business service that the emerging legal marijuana industry doesn't need. The sky is really the limit when it comes to skilled service providers offering cannabis businesses top-rate services and specialty products.

During this exciting time of rapid expansion of medical (and now recreational) marijuana "free states", you can make a very good living finding your service or product niche. You can even let the cannabis-handling growers, dispensaries, edibles companies, testing labs, and other firms that directly handle marijuana pay you to handle the many aspects of business that aren't about touching the green stuff.

You may also be completely comfortable launching a growing, dispensing, retailing, or edibles operation that requires you to handle marijuana and make decisions about the manner and degree to which you will comply with the boat-loads of emerging regulations for such businesses. The financial rewards are generally very lucrative, and getting in at this early stage of legalization has many benefits for those willing to jump in now, while the cannabis business landscape is still developing.

Retail opportunities, ranging from dispensaries to cannabis-friendly bed and breakfast inns to bakeries, are all expanding, opening soon, or on the drawing board for innovators with an eye for opportunities and untapped profitable markets.

Cannabis businesses are searching for professional services that respect the ways that the highly regulated legal marijuana business market requires specialty expertise. But, mostly, cannabis-focused business owners report that they want professionalism from their vendors, and are perfectly happy to help vendors incorporate specific local or state requirements if the overall knowledge and service level is high.

This book is focused on providing aspiring cannabis business entrepreneurs with specific ideas, strategies, and context for starting a profitable business—by designing the business specifically to meet the needs of some part of the legal marijuana market.

If you already offer legal, tax, medical, or other credentialed professional services, you can certainly profit by welcoming clients who are in the legal marijuana business sector. We have provided marketing advice here that will help any business targeting the cannabusiness industry. But our next book, "Marketing Professional Services to the Cannabis Industry", may be a better fit for established businesses who are not evaluating business opportunities, but instead are seeking ways to successfully expand by framing their existing professional services practice, technology company, or real estate venture in ways attractive and responsive to the needs of the marijuana industry and business community.

One advantage of offering business services to the cannabis industry is that most business plans in this category have substantially lower legal risks than businesses that handle marijuana directly.

If you are at all worried that your mother-in-law, adult kids, existing customers (assuming you are already in business) or banker may look askance at your new cannabis clientele—go ahead and set up a separate brand, and in many cases, a separate LLC or other corporate entity to serve your new market. It's smart to keep your marijuana-focused business fully separate from any other income or assets. You'll likely want to consult a qualified attorney to double check your plans.

Wait a minute, you're saying! I'm not a real estate pro, an HR veteran, a marketing and sales maven. Security is not my bag, and I've never baked a cookie without burning it. Stay tuned. There are so many profitable opportunities that we believe you'll find your niche in the marijuana business boom yet.

No matter what your special skills, you can find the right opportunity to build a highly profitable business—teaching others what you know, or making something that marijuana businesses can retail. Realize that business opportunities can be tailored to accommodate your available start-up capital, your current location, a need to start part-time, or other factors.

Certainly having some working capital is essential to many businesses, but our suggestions are biased toward enterprises that can be started incrementally. We are especially excited about opportunities in the emerging legal marijuana business that can be started, very realistically, with little more than pocket change.

Let's talk about the services and products that are selling now, and how you can get your share of the legal-marijuana Green Rush!

Human Resources

MARIJUANA RETAILERS—WHETHER DISPENSARIES, CLUBS or recreational shops —need training in how to hire, train, and motivate employees. They need, and are happy to pay for, human resources compliance advice that you may think is pretty basic. You probably have some expertise if you have experience in a company of any size's human resources department.

You may know the ins and outs of the Americans with Disabilities Act (ADA) and how those requirements may apply to employees who themselves are medical marijuana patients. Policies around when and if employees are allowed to keep their medicine at work, and whether they are allowed to medicate while on the job, are developing areas.

Your business should be able to attract dispensary and other cannabis industry clients who want to make certain that they are on the right side of legal regulations, while at the same time able to recruit and retain valuable employees that already understand the benefits of medical marijuana.

Personnel forms, legal and not-legal interview questions, benefits conversations, scheduling systems, and even post-firing exit interview practices, are likely all new to your cannabis business owner. As an outsourced **HR director**, or consultant, you can provide your advice by the hour, day, or week.

Human resources is also another area where the opportunity to market books, ebooks, videos, webinars, and even kits of necessary forms or policy manuals, offer substantial revenue opportunities. These ancillary offerings also can help establish you as an expert when marketing your consulting services.

Start-up costs for human resource related services companies should be well under $5000. If need be, you can truly start on a shoe-string (perhaps while keeping your day job) in this category because there are no requirements for licensing, training, certification, or location.

Of course, you may need a local business license but first get out there and market your services to a client or two.

Staffing Services & Events

THE FIRST STAFFING AND RECRUITING **agencies** for marijuana-focused businesses are already in business, and making money. If you have the experience to help match businesses with well-paying jobs to qualified people seeking those jobs, the staffing industry may be the perfect marijuana niche for you.

Risks and start-up costs are low in this category, as no one in your business needs to handle marijuana and there are few required, fixed licensure or other costs to getting started.

Medical marijuana dispensaries, and recreational stores, as well as edibles companies, growers, companies that market services to any of these markets, all need qualified people to work in their businesses. They want people who understand that their business is a business and that there is no job title "stoner" to be had.

Your role will be to help the hiring businesses develop professional job descriptions for positions ranging from trimmers in the greenhouse to budtenders in the dispensary, to data management specialists in the medical marijuana doctor's back office, to executive management.

Each job will of course have specialized qualifications. Someone qualified to be a recreational budtender will need customer service skills and hopefully already have some knowledge of strains and other marijuana product knowledge. The employer will also want to validate, in some way, that their new budtender is not going to steal, or act unprofessionally.

Executive jobs may have requirements for both past business experience and the ability to make investor presentations as well as marketing, grow experience, compliance qualifications, or other skill sets required for the particular position.

You'll often be asked to fill executive jobs on contingency, earning your money as a percentage of the hired person's salary. The fee will be paid by the employer, generally after a probationary period of 30–90 days.

Non-executive positions, whether in the growing segment or in retail or edibles manufacturing, are more likely to be hourly positions. You'll have to decide whether your business model is contingency based, or more likely based on marking up the hourly wage of employees to cover your fees.

In some states and markets you may find it very profitable to offer **payroll** and other HR services bundled with your employee recruitment and hiring services. Because many direct handling marijuana businesses have expensive and/or difficult banking relationships, your payroll services should be marked up to fully reflect the value of those services within the industry.

Another staffing related service is **background checking** and/or employee drug testing. Now before you laugh out loud, consider this: Marijuana-industry employers, especially in manufacturing or delivery categories, may be required to comply with "drug free workplace" rules by the Federal Department of Transportation, OSHA, or other authorities. Your pre-employment testing and background checking may be permitted, by your client, to have higher tolerance for marijuana related activities. But you, as the neutral third party, will profit by taking the background investigation of key hires, and/or the drug testing of employees where testing is required, off the plate of the business owner.

Part of staffing or background checking services, in some states, will be to walk the new employee through any required state registration, training, or licensure.

Another potentially very profitable business niche—whether run by staffing services or as an independent events production company—is **specialty job fairs** and other related events.

Fairs and events can either be structured to meet the hiring and recruitment needs of particular employers or sub-industries like retail dispensaries or growers. Or job fairs can be offered to the general job-seeking public, with attendees and exhibiting employers paying a fee to participate.

One enterprising entrepreneur has produced at least one job fair offering medical marijuana patients the opportunity to meet friendly employers, in numerous industries who need highly motivated and loyal workers and see medical cannabis patients as an applicant pool that they may have overlooked in the past. For the medical marijuana patients, applying for jobs without having to decide between disclosing or not disclosing their medical marijuana patient status was well worth the $10.00 admission.

Early results from job fairs in Colorado and Washington show strong response from both employers and job-seekers. You can very profitably organize, publicize, and profit from several job fairs each year. And the opportunities for expanding into sub-industry specific events, such as grower and greenhouse jobs, and edibles is largely untapped, currently.

Plants, growing, horticulture

IF YOU CAN LEAD A horticulture...**teach a class**!

Horticulture knowledge is easily found in books. And the medical marijuana industry has a long history of great experts, like Ed Rosenthal, graciously sharing their knowledge of every step in the cultivation process via books, lectures and even videos.

The good news is you don't have to be well-known, like Ed, or have his encyclopedic knowledge to be able to offer valuable training to the hordes of newbies flooding into the industry. Many available resources start way over the heads, knowledge-wise, of new entrants into the field.

You are going to profit best by meeting your students where they are, not skipping over the basics that, "everyone already knows." At Oaksterdam Unversity and other established marijuana-industry training and education centers, many students are retired couples, just-say-no generation career changers, and others who are sincere when they reveal that they know nothing about the topic they are now studying.

Whether you are teaching a course on organic horticulture techniques or how to craft hand crème, you'll want to make sure you assess your audience and start at the beginning.

Sustainable and organic cultivation improvement: These growers know marijuana, speak about clones and strains like a foreign language, but many are scaling operations from their former underground businesses in foil lined closets. They need to know how to apply the kinds of operational procedures used by nurseries and market organic farmers.

If you know about organic pest control, start there. A You tube video (or ten), a website or blog, offering to give a talk at your local medical marijuana club, daily Twitter tips, and before long you will have gained a following and be able to grow business opportunities. Many growers could use a knowledgeable consultant on how to gain the upper hand over spider mites and other opportunistic critters, without harming the crop or introducing chemicals into the organic environment.

Poo is profitable too.

ZooPoo is as you probably guessed the composted dung of a certain Western US zoo. The zoo has made a very nice side income for over 25 years by bagging up the composted ZooPoo and selling it to a grateful and amused public. The fact that marijuana grows are interested in organic farming techniques and could easily gain marketing benefits by using ZooPoo, or your home-made organic fertilizer tea, is an opportunity that has profit, written in dirt, all over it.

Energy for the Future

BUGS NOT YOUR BAG? HOW about teaching growers how to maximize production while minimizing water and electricity use. So much the better if you know about **solar installation** or **automatic watering systems**.

Energy is Big Business; saving energy is profitable. Lighting, ventilation, air conditioning, and de-humidification comprise 80% of a typical growing operation's monthly energy bill. This runs into thousands of dollars every month for each of the estimated 2000 commercial level growing operations in place currently in legal medical marijuana states.

Lots of companies offer more and more efficient lighting, and you might decide that's your niche as well. Colorado's mega-energy company, Xcel, has reported that 1/2 − 1% of energy the company generated in Colorado currently is used to grow marijuana. That's a lot of megawatts and a huge basket of potential profits for entrepreneurs who can help growers pay less of their overall take to Xcel.

But in the coming boom years, profits are going to build fast for businesses that can tackle the huge energy bills of growers in other areas, like air conditioning and ventilation.

One company we know installs air conditioning efficiency improvements right up on the roof of their clients. They don't want to serve the legal marijuana industry. They prefer cutting the power bills of big box stores and commercial nurseries.

Start-up costs for bidding on and then installing **energy use efficiency systems**, monitoring devices that turn down units when conditions allow, and other related HVAC technology is readily available to many markets, but a brand new opportunity for you to introduce to commercial marijuana grow operations.

Solar and small-scale wind power are quickly going to become essential equipment as commercial growers expand and see their power bills soar. Whether motivated by potential cost savings, marketing benefits for growing 'green' weed, or a nudge from the local utility in the form of high use surcharges or even usage throttling, growers will be investing in alternative power solutions.

Another business option is **HVAC and grow system maintenance** and repair. Every grow has fussy equipment that runs everything from lights, to watering, to air conditioning, to dehumidification. Each piece of equipment will eventually need repair or upgrade. If you have anywhere from handyman to expert solar or wind tech skills, a profitable business, with very low start-up costs can be found by being the guy or gal who fixes the leaking waterer or the failed fan system.

Information Please

BLACK THUMB? HOW ABOUT TEACHING local edibles companies food safety rules that you learned working in your state's restaurant or food manufacturing industry. Several growing businesses, for now concentrated in Colorado, offer **seminars**, **trainings**, and **site surveys** for marijuana edibles companies in order to help them meet emerging food inspection standards and food handling regulations.

Workshops, videos, online products and Amazon Kindle books are all profitable ways to share knowledge that you may think is something "everyone knows," that is actually vital to growing cannabis businesses who are just now becoming subject to standard food safety and food handling requirements. Price your services fairly and don't forget to offer individual consulting to companies facing a list of to-fix items after a failed inspection or upcoming requirements to improve their food handling systems.

In this same area, one enterprising young woman we know is writing customized food handling and procedures manuals for edibles companies. She charges for her consulting time as well as a well crafted binder with full procedures, MSDS sheets for cleaning items, check lists, etc. She certainly hasn't won the financial lottery yet, but she did make enough in 2014 to quit her day job as a kitchen manager at a hotel.

You can win big in online and traditional **publishing** during the current legalization fueled Green Boom. It helps if you already know what a media kit is, and what it should contain, but even if you are a total publishing newbie, profit potential is huge in publishing.

One of our favorite online publications is Ladybud. They say they are "classing up the joint." They also say, off the record, that they have entertained multiple offers to sell the online magazine and that most of their advertisers call them to buy space or a sponsorship.

One of the things LadyBud has going for it is a genuine and unique editorial voice. The mag covers marijuana news, exposes scams as they see them, runs really high-end gourmet recipes and also addresses broader social issues. This is not High Times and you'll never find what one of our friends in the advertising business calls 'bong porn' in their socially conscious pages.

Your publication idea may be a socially conservative venue for gun lovers to hang together online. I won't read it but there may be an audience and now is the time to scope out your editorial point of view and gain traffic and traction—while interest is high and even market leaders have to share the road, and advertising revenue, with newcomers.

WeedMaps, a guide to dispensary locations, meant to be searched on your smartphone, makes solid claims to at least 18 million dollars of revenue a year, and likely enjoys much higher revenue; it has been the cutest girl at the merger and acquisition ball twice, already. These guys say that they are the "Yelp" of the legal marijuana community and maybe they are. Folks we talk to generally think of them as a **map**, and let us know that the additional site features leave plenty of room for would-be competitors.

There are opportunities for upstart **regional publications** to offer news, features, maps, and of course advertising to their local dispensary and user community.

Dispensaries really want local reach advertising because, at least for now, they are fenced out of Google's ever popular adWords, and really don't want to pay the national rates of the big magazines and online publications just to reach patients along Ventura Boulevard in California. Colorado Springs dispensaries resist advertising that runs in Denver and Boulder for the same reason: it doesn't provide a critical mass of narrowly targeted readers.

In addition to the many profitable possibilities in general, or consumer, publications, there are also buckets of real money to be made in creating **business to business publications** for various legal marijuana market niches. Before long edibles companies, specialty glass blowers, marijuana friendly doctors, recreational store owners, and a long list of other niche participants will visit and subscribe to specialty publications tailored just for them.

Doctors will want news that matters to them about insurance, regulatory changes, patient evaluation models, technology solutions, and other information directly relevant to their service within the legal marijuana professional community. They will not want human interest stories making health claims and will have no interest in merchandising ideas for retail stores.

Edibles companies will want to be kept up to date on regulations and innovations in the areas of packaging, dosing, technology, and an ever changing list of topics that would, quite frankly, bore a non baker/cook to tears.

The beauty of online based publications is that you can pivot and re-target as your customers (advertisers) and readers evolve and let you know what they most want to see and read.

But what should I charge? Do some online research to see what competitors, or even similar publications in different industries, are charging. These days the publication media kit is almost always online. Google a publication name and "media kit" and you'll likely have a good start for your market research.

Design your publication for your advertisers and your readers and also keep an eye out for the add-on opportunities that you can offer. One well-known publisher offers specialty reports and puts on conferences that appeal to their target market. Both reports and conferences are heavily advertised in the online publication and provide multiple options for advertisers to buy exposure to a market they very much want to reach.

Security Related

A HUGE AMOUNT OF SECURITY expertise is needed, in every corner of the marijuana industry: from grower to retailer, to dispensary, to home delivery of medicines to patients.

Security and Loss Control Audits

Our friend Chuck has made a very nice six-figure income by offering security and loss control audits to growers and dispensaries. When Chuck comes through the door he immediately sees the easy-to-snatch, expensive hand-blown delivery devices too close to the door for his taste. He goes positively ballistic when he sees employee exits without standard precautions to deter even great employees from succumbing to the temptation to help themselves to a little take-home bonus.

In addition to the obvious theft magnets of marijuana, cash, and retail products, Chuck also protects his clients by providing a full security audit so that they don't lose their shirts by having employees help themselves to gasoline, meant for company generators and vehicles, office supplies, growing mediums, spare parts, discarded lighting systems, display cases, basically anything that isn't nailed down. Chuck is very clear that cannabis focused owners are likely to under value the potential losses of anything they have on their premises that isn't marijuana or cash.

Chuck learned his trade at a huge electronics big-box store and does not have a degree in teaching people how to not get ripped off. Many of his best methods were learned watching big boxes walk out the back door of big stores. He's a great example of using the skills you already have to build a very profitable business, by framing your expertise to solve the problems that all businesses face—with a nod to the special, extra challenges that the newly legal marijuana industry must address in order to profit and grow.

Security is complicated for marijuana handling businesses because in addition to the obvious value of the marijuana (in every form) current banking issues make the businesses virtually 100% cash businesses. This is likely to change as states and the federal government allow banks to work with legal cannabis businesses routinely. Until then, buckets of cash lying around the back office of a dispensary are common, and dangerous on many levels.

Disappearing cash can obviously bankrupt the business, but it can also leave gaps between heavily regulated tracking of cash and product, threatening licensure or even legal status. Those same stacks of twenties are also a formidable temptation to anyone who might decide to help themselves to some of the spoils. Chuck helps dispensaries design ways to track those stacks and make sure that cash is not an attractive nuisance to insiders or outsiders who might target the business.

Chuck's security business is focused on eyeballing the premises and making written and verbal recommendations for ways that the business can lower loss potential and better monitor security targets within the business. Other security businesses are much more focused on muscle and technology.

Video security

Video cameras, with data capture, are a standard (often required) feature of growing operations and most dispensaries. If you know how the video cameras should be spaced and wired, there are profits waiting for you. If you know how to wire it all together with easy web-based data storage and on-demand viewing, you will set yourself above many people currently selling into some dispensary and grow markets.

Chuck and other security consultants would like to refer your first customers because they freely admit, "I'm not a tech guy." Camera monitoring technology and web-based surveillance systems are a very profitable part of the marijuana market and buyers understand that these systems are required for regulatory compliance, not just to keep sticky fingers honest.

You can begin small and build your business on referrals. A background in alarm systems, video systems, even automobile sound systems will get you started. Start-up costs are reasonable for most technology-based security companies. You can use a laptop for demos that most manufacturers have online and order on an as needed basis, without stocking equipment before sale. We have seen these systems installed out of a Corolla so a big truck and lots of tools, rolls of cable, etc. are nice-to-haves, rather than essential start-up equipment.

Alarms and Access Control

Whether a grow operation, dispensary, head shop, or retail store, all marijuana industry businesses need alarm systems and access control for their premises. Many operations currently share growing functions on the same property with a dispensary, and must tightly control who is allowed access to different areas of the operation.

What may seem like a simple door access control project to you, if you have even basic experience in the alarm industry, is a really important security priority for business owners who must comply not only with security concerns, but also regulatory requirements around who may enter the medical marijuana dispensary, grow area, or retail head shop. Start-up costs are reasonable with many security companies starting for under $10,000 and some bootstrapping their way up from $2000-$5000.

Bouncers, Guards, and Big Guys

Big guys are an opportunity in security too: we know of one bouncer for rent business serving Southern California dispensaries very profitably. We are told there is plenty of room for more businesses specializing in onsite security staffing.

If you have "a presence" as they call it in the bouncer hiring business, and any sort of background that will give customers confidence that you will keep things calm, not look for conflict, and if you are bondable, you may find yourself with more customers than you and the buddies you recruit can handle. Just remember that your job, and that of anyone you hire, is to prevent problems, and you're getting paid to notice things.

Marketing, Sales & Promotion

WERE YOU THE WINDOW DECORATING wizard at Urban Outfitter? The social marketing goddess at a local business? Did you serve time as part of the marketing or sales army of a retailer or technology company? Did you sell Girl Scout cookies more creatively than anyone else in troop 435? Have you been building web sites since you were in middle school? Can you create an app that a dispensary can give its patients to check on daily specials and menu items?

Every marijuana business, from direct growers to retailers to providers of professional services, all share one thing in common: They need **marketing, sales, sales operations, and merchandising consulting** so that their business avoids mistakes and maximizes profits with techniques, promotions, merchandising, marketing materials, and sales strategies that are well planned and profitable.

Lots of companies are rushing into the cannabis green rush offering consulting that tries to be all things to all businesses. Our suggestion, based on talking with real live cannabusiness owners, is to pick a specific area where you can make a difference and demonstrate how following your suggestions in your area of expertise increases profits for your clients, and stick to that specialty. Once you have a profitable client base and some good referrals, then of course, add services, expand, grow.

In many areas, sales and marketing tasks among them, the line between training your cannabusiness clients how to do tasks, and simply selling them the service of outsourcing web site administration, or HR functions, or payroll, is one where you'll often have the option of choosing how much service versus consulting you want to provide.

Marijuana business owners spend an average of 1.3 days each week on regulatory and compliance matters in the newly legalized states of Colorado and Washington. You can pretty much bet that in many cases owners and management would rather pay you to DO the task than to take the time to learn what you have to teach them that would enable them to do various tasks themselves.

Real Estate services

DISPENSARY OWNERS ARE CONSTANTLY WORRIED about real estate related issues. For good reason.

Dispensary Janitorial

Rob wants an honest janitorial service that he can trust to do nightly cleaning of patient and office areas of his dispensary building. He would ideally like to have the same team have a crew that could do basic housekeeping for the nearby grow area but he feels that few dispensary owners would allow contractors into the grow area. He has tried calling various janitorial services and been quoted shockingly high rates, once the vendor hears that they're bidding on a dispensary that they presume to be rolling in cash. He's also been refused bids by companies who aren't ready to be associated with a legal, tax-paying marijuana business just yet. Rob has gotten by hiring dispensary patients on a piece-meal basis.

Your professional, targeted to medical or professional offices, cleaning service would be a welcome load off Rob's mind. Please don't forget to dust the silk ficus in the lobby and wipe down the water cooler.

Landlord and real estate referral service

Several cannabusiness owners wished that there were a referral service, online directory, or other service for locating marijuana-friendly landlords for commercial real estate locations. Yes, in some cases the federal government has sent letters to landlords warning against renting to marijuana businesses. But those days have virtually ended (except in Southern California where a whole different dynamic makes landlord/tenant situations difficult right now).

No one we know in the industry wants to rent random houses for grows, like they used to. They are happy to pay referral fees, somewhat above-market rents to compensate the landlord for any risks or hassles they might encounter, and have no problem paying deposits to protect their landlord against any losses. If you can prescreen for business owners who are ready and willing to partner with marijuana related businesses, both sides of the deal will happily pay you to take the hassles and uncertainty out of the deal.

Cannabis Location Scout / Realtor

If you are a realtor and can identify properties that meet local dispensary location rules, find friendly property management companies for technology and other businesses that serve the direct growers and retailers, you may be able to ignore the next housing bubble. Finally, if you are a property owner, consider letting cannabusiness tenants know that you are industry friendly.

Medical-marijuana-friendly residential landlord

On the residential side, we have direct and very profitable knowledge that letting local dispensaries know you are a medical marijuana-friendly landlord will virtually ensure that you will never lack for tenants. Let those tenants have a well-behaved pet and you are likely to have a waiting list for units, years into the future.

Bakeries, Snack Foods, and other Goodies

ONE OF THE BIGGEST SURPRISES of the legal marijuana industry is just how hot, hot, hot, edible products are in every market. The market for infused edibles is one of the fastest growing segments of the cannabis and medical marijuana market.

One of the most frequent concerns expressed by dispensary owners is the constant challenge of keeping enough edibles in stock. With somewhere North of 1.4 million medical marijuana patients in states with medical marijuana dispensaries, and a rapidly expanding number of recreational customers with recent legalization, the infused edibles market is on the grow. Estimates of the size of the edibles market are widely divergent and lack the kind of statistical validation that banks and investors might like to see. But, $600 million dollars is the lowest figure we've seen for 2014 and many industry watchers and bean counters come up with up to $900 million as the 2014 number.

That's a lot of lollipops, cookies, caramels, sodas, hard candies, sauces, etc. Especially when you look at the relatively tiny number of edibles companies currently in business. Industry estimates, again less reliable than we'd like, all agree that there are currently less than 1000 edibles companies in operation. But there will be more tomorrow.

Currently your primary market for infused edibles is primarily the 2500+ dispensaries already in business across the country. But several hundred new dispensaries are opening this year, and more states have added medical and recreational dispensaries as a result of 2014 elections so even without interstate expansion opportunities, your market is growing.

Your state market may be start small, if you are selling already medicated products to your state medical and/or recreational market. State lines still largely control where and how much business you can do with your infused products business. Location matters for products with the active THC ingredient baked into the metaphorical cake. But interest and demand are huge.

Infused, or medicated, food items are purchased by over 70% of shoppers at medical and recreational retail establishments. These products are infused with varying quantities of THC, the active marijuana buzz, as well as other cannabis based elements (Like CBDs) that are considered to have medicinal benefits beyond the THC buzz.

From infused lollipops, to the classic brownie, to delivered to your door meal kits with an add-your-own-herb kick, to sodas, energy drinks, granola, spaghetti sauce, and even medicated kale chips, there isn't an edible item that hasn't flown off dispensary shelves. Estimates from a few dispensary owners, not all in Colorado, suggest that about 30% – 40% of total cannabis sales are infused edibles, when consumers and patients have a selection of edibles available.

It's pretty easy to see why edibles are so popular: they are the best example of two very strong preferences and trends among cannabis and medical marijuana consumers:

Customers/ patients are increasingly unwilling to smoke. Face it, most people have moved on from smoky bars, restaurants, even casinos are going smoke-free. It's lousy for your lungs and makes you smell like a cannabis ashtray.

Second, today's recreational cannabis users and medical marijuana patients are adults who prefer taking their medicine, or enjoying their recreational buzz, discreetly. Even among those who vaporize or otherwise inhale, discreet delivery devices are the fastest growing category of what was formerly known as paraphenalia.

In some states where medical dispensaries are forbidden, by law, from selling smokeable cannabis, edibles opportunities are showing what's ahead in other states as fewer and fewer people are willing to smoke anything. For any reason.

Your grandma's butterscotch chip cookie recipe may well be your ticket to winning in the green rush. Or maybe you have the vegan caramel power bar that will create lines out the door. Sure there are some well-capitalized brands that want to become the Starbucks of infused chocolates, but no company has leadership right now. There is still plenty of room for you and your edibles plan to take off.

One of our favorite edibles strategies involves making fabulous treats and then packaging them so that the dispensary can add the active THC concentrate, in the store, from their licensed inventory, and keep you in the clear when shipping etc. While giving the dispensary better product, more reliable supplies, and adhering strictly to most local laws which require tight sourcing of the actual cannabis ingredient and highly localized package labeling, onsite infusion is far less work for the dispensary than baking cookies in someone's kitchen.

Start-up costs: Edibles businesses can have start-up costs ranging from a few hundred dollars to multiple hundreds of thousands invested by companies setting up fancy packaging and automated production facilities now, in hopes that they will become the Hershey's of cannabis-infused chocolate when they can expand to multiple states.

Again, good statistics, including the ones sold for big bucks by consulting and media firms, are pretty much guesses. But leaving out individual dispensaries baking cookies in a toaster oven on the back room, and solo cooks working from home, start-up costs seem to stay under $10,000 for most edibles company start-ups, with over half reporting they spend less than $5000, initially. Costs are lower in less-regulated states like California where packaging is not regulated and licensure and tax rules are still in development. Marketing costs are also lower in the less regulated states because dispensaries are not yet used to high-end razzle-dazzle presentations, samples, and displays. Nor are the biggest brands interested in risking a large display system and inventory in states where dispensaries are perceived as not as stable as the "free states."

Super states like Colorado and Washington have added expensive packaging, labeling, testing, and food handling related costs, as well as eye-popping licensure fees and taxes, that quickly move start-up costs into the $10,000 – $50,000 range for even pretty modest operations. We have successful friends who have built a very profitable Colorado edibles company with far less cash but they are becoming the exception thanks to ever growing legal and licensing costs. The rewards can be huge, with a few investor funded edibles companies reporting revenues over 6 million dollars per year.

Of course, as in every case where statistics in our new industry are reported, a skeptical eye should raise at least one eye brow when such huge early profits are reported. A more reasonable figure for a small edibles start-up, not a solo home kitchen operation, but one with minimal equipment and infrastructure investment is likely to clock in at closer to $200,000-$300,000 in annual revenue. If you are a solo operator with limited products and limited costs, your edibles business is likely to net under $100,000 in annual revenue and that may be just great compared to your old cake-decorating gig.

Arts & Inventions

ARTISTS AND ARTISANS ARE IN **strong demand**

Cannabis and medical-marijuana culture is growing and maturing as it becomes more and more mainstream. The art around marijuana has come a long way since the concert and High Times posters of my youth.

No matter what your art, you will need to either develop the research and sales skills to show your work to potential wholesale or retail customers, or partner with someone who finds the sales and marketing aspects of your art a great fit with their skills. You might consider taking a course through your community college or state arts organization on the business of art, and arts marketing. Some professional coaching on marketing is particularly helpful if your sales efforts, up until now, have been giving away your work in trade for, umm, whatever.

Jewelry

Beautiful art, like that created at Silverkind, is worn with pride by people who have benefited from medical marijuana or simply like the beautiful and meticulously crafted designs. Look at that pink ribbon necklace, worn by the older woman at your Y, closely, and you may find a subtle nod to the medical marijuana that helped her along her road to healing.

Glass, wood work, and other marijuana-delivery tools

Glass blowers in several states create Chihuly-worthy pipes and vaporizers that can sell for thousands of dollars. Some glass artists have developed enough of a following that their smoke wares are considered too valuable to use and stand untarnished by marijuana, in places of honor in art collections and homes. Wood workers are creating some of the cutting edge, discreet delivery devices, that are among the highest demand paraphenalia.

Graphic Designers

Graphic designers are creating art but they are also building the brand identities of hundreds of industry start-ups. Web designers who create professional, yet exciting, sites have work backed up. Your art may be used by businesses, sold at cannabis festivals and events, sold or displayed at retailers, and much more.

Head shops, and stores focused on vaping and e-cigarette delivery systems, are growing. This is true even though many head and smoke shops worried about loss of business once dispensaries arrived on the scene and carrying various items that are useful or simply beautiful. It turns out there is plenty of business to go around and both retail cannabis seller and traditional smoke and head shops are actively seeking out more and better inventory to get their share of the rejuvenated industry.

Inventor

One of my favorite inventions is a percalator-type kettle that allows the processing of marijuana and butter into the Cannabutter needed for yummy cooking. What makes it so special? The inventors came up with ways to keep the smell of buttery, but undeniably stinky, marijuana from wafting throughout the cooks home, dorm room, or other smell sensitive kitchen location. It may sound like a small invention but it's becoming big business because lots and lots of legal users do not want, or cannot have, the strong smell of cooking herb in their living space.

Discreet Delivery Device inventor

The number one, top selling, mentioned in every survey, product winner of 2014 was discreet marijuana delivery devices. If you can invent vape, e-cig, lozenge, or other devices that make administration of medicinal or recreational cannabis more discreet for users, you will profit.

The fastest growing category of inventory demand in the head/ smoke shop/paraphenalia industry is constant, growing user demand for discreet and easy to use delivery devices. We fifty year-olds did not keep the bongs of the 80's and are not very likely to roll a joint and light up. The industry is scrambling to fill their shelves with grown-up, well made, discrete delivery and storage items that don't look or act like they belong in a teenager's basement kid-cave. If you have the craftsmanship or invention skills to fill a shelf with equipment that serves the purpose of safely and subtly delivering the medicinal or recreational marijuana dose to today's average user, who is 45 and as likely to be female as not, you have profits waiting for you at the next wholesale show. Take some samples by your local shops and you may have all the orders you can handle.

The head shop industry and its cousin the smoke shop/e-cigarette shop has annual wholesale buyers shows where much shopping and stocking is done. If you want to scale your art related business, you'll likely want to hook into one or more of the trade associations and their publications and events.

http://www.hqmag.com/ and http://erbmagazine.com/ are a couple of good online magazines to get you started. Both feature articles and buyers guides, as well as many advertisers, that will give you a good idea of what folks in the retail head shop and smoke shop space are looking for in new vendors.

Don't forget, when putting together your marketing plan, that lots of very high quality cannabis-themed art is turning up on Etsy as well as in retail and event locations not necessarily devoted solely to the cannabis crowd.

Lotions, Potions, Topicals

FOR A DIFFERENT KIND OF art, your road to profit may be in creating creams, salves, and other **artisanal topical preparations**. This is another area where you may find your niche creating the base, and letting the dispensaries add active ingredients (as some state laws would require), or you may be able to create the pain relief and other benefits that many patients are seeking with topical creations, infused with THC or other hemp based ingredients.

We list this category here in the artistic and invention area because packaging of topical THC is much less regulated than edibles. Your elegant, whimsical, or other well-designed packaging is likely to make a huge impact on how easy it is for you to place your products in retail locations, or even how well you'll sell at the local farmer's or craft market.

Caregiving, home services, & delivery

CAREGIVING IS AT THE HEART of the medical marijuana movement. Each patient represents someone who believes that medical marijuana will help heal their illness, or at least alleviate their pain.

Yes, it's true there is a wide range among patients utilizing dispensaries. Some are sick, suffering from illnesses and symptoms of a magnitude that means these people need additional caregiving services beyond simple access to marijuana. It is also true that you may not immediately know just how much the apparently healthy young man you see at the dispensary is suffering from PTSD or another invisible, but qualifying, condition under the state's medical marijuana legalization legislation.

Do I think there are perfectly healthy people who have used the system to gain access to marijuana, for purely recreational use? Who cares what my opinion is, or yours? And so what. In the end most of us agree that prohibition should end and reasonable regulation implemented over marijuana. Period.

So with the 'But are the medical patients really sick?' argument behind us, let's focus on the fact that there are a variety of very good business opportunities available for people with genuine caregiving skills and motivation.

In certain parts of the country, Southern California in particular, many medical marijuana businesses are delivery-only. They deliver medicine to qualified patients. This may be an option for you if you have the start-up resources and know-how to build a **mobile dispensary**. Additional services such as home care assistance, grocery shopping and delivery, housekeeping, errands, and transportation to doctors or other appointments are natural add-ons to a delivery-based medical marijuana dispensary.

If you live in an area where delivery is not permitted, you can still provide much needed caregiving services to medical marijuana patients by advertising through local dispensaries and partnering with marijuana-friendly doctors to gain access, and even referrals, to patients who genuinely need **in-home care services** for themselves, and often their pets.

Knowing that you, the medical-marijuana-friendly **dog walker** and **errand service** provider are available, and not someone who will look sideways at signs of medicine in the house, can be very reassuring for customers, and provide the basis for a profitable business for you.

It is likely best to specialize based on your interests, skills, and any home care, nursing, massage, vet tech, or other qualifications and certifications. Many medical marijuana patients prefer not to drive while on high-dose medicine and may need only errand shopping services. Others need a genuine home health provider with varied skill levels.

You can start where you are comfortable with very few start-up costs, beyond brochures and business cards, and add other services and even other people, with additional skills, as your business grows.

Hot or frozen meal delivery is another caregiving service that many patients will gladly pay a very fair price for. We are speaking here only of non-medicated meals. Edibles are another topic completely. But if you can tailor meals available to the health and dietary requests of your patient community, your business will be popular and profitable.

Check those local regulations and study up on food safety basics if you are going to focus on food. Depending on where you live you may be exempt from local health department regulations as a "cottage industry" exempt operator. Or you may live in health department aggressive land, where you'll need to move up to building meals in a rented or borrowed commercial kitchen before Dot the health department lady gets word of your glowing reviews and growing success.

Services in the caregiving category tend to be low to no start-up cost, but do require you to put yourself out there to market your services and let dispensaries, patients, doctors, and other caregiving businesses hear the news that you have set up shop and are ready, willing, and able to provide your particular menu of services to the medical marijuana community.

Profits can be very good in caregiving businesses if you can avoid the usual care giver tendency of under-charging, or giving away too much of your valuable time and services. Caregivers are special and you do need to make money. Don't feel bad about charging a fair rate for your housekeeping, dog walking, transport, meals, or other care related services. Your clients will be happy to pay fair prices and they don't want to see you go out of business because you gave too much away.

Testing labs and analysis

TESTING LABS ARE A VERY profitable business, and are gaining popularity as states mandate testing for cannabis and other naturally occurring compounds in all legally grown and processed marijuana. Retailers and consumers, both medical and recreational, are more and more interested in the exact potency of the product they are selling and/or using. As other compounds found in marijuana, besides the well-known THC, are linked to treatment for various ailments and alleviation of symptoms, THC (the compound noted for creating the marijuana high) is only the tip of the testing iceberg.

Different marijuana strains have differing levels of dozens of compounds. Independent testing labs, and even labs within dispensaries, are growing quickly as interest and regulation of this testing grows.

Edibles and other manufacturers also need to know the composition and strength of their ingredients for accurate dosing and raw ingredient selection.

Finally, testing for various contaminants is a growing area of consumer concern and dispensaries are feeling pressure from their patients and customers to show testing results that show a mold-free, pesticide-free, extraction-agent-free product (butane for

Contaminant testing

example in concentrates). In other words, consumers want their marijuana to be as clean as their organic groceries and lab testing showing a "clean" product is very reassuring.

No one knows the exact size of the testing market for all of the usual reasons, plus the fact that some marijuana is being tested quietly, in labs that do not acknowledge, much less advertise, their participation in the cannabis testing industry.

On the records there are under twenty labs currently active, with about the same number projected to come online in 2015–16. These numbers will change rapidly if inter-state movement of marijuana becomes less legally risky. Or if additional states add testing requirements that justify someone investing in additional testing facility development in that state.

Right now $20 million dollars in annual revenue is a frequently repeated guesstimate of the testing industry revenue and that is expected to grow with increased testing focused regulations. This number reflects reluctance on the part of many cannabusiness owners to spend precious capital on testing unless or until it is mandated by law. These same businesses point to a lack of standardization and oversight within the testing field as another reason why consumers and regulators should limit testing requests and requirements.

Labs themselves have some reluctance to build out fully iterated systems, no matter how profitable current services are, because rapidly changing regulations might leave them holding the bag on sunk investment costs for outdated equipment. They know that changes to the whole testing environment could create the need to acquire expensive new equipment, or higher educational credentials for trained staff, in order to comply with regulations that as of now have not been announced, or even contemplated.

Starting a testing lab is a great business idea for anyone with the skills to operate the expensive analyzers necessary to produce useable results. You might be surprised how few letters you need after your name to successfully own and operate a testing lab. Equipment is sophisticated and does much of the actual science.

Currently it is unrealistic to plan on start-up costs for a lab, from scratch, with under $200,000 available for equipment, licensing, etc. If you happen to be lucky enough to already own or have access to a laboratory focused on agricultural testing, you may be able to start a business focused on limited testing for grower contaminants such as mold and pesticides for far less investment.

If you can get the start-up costs and have some expertise, the chance of bringing high-six-figure annual revenue from your marijuana testing lab is very high. Few labs report losing money and most (over 90%) are on as rapid a growth path as current equipment capacity and local regulatory challenges allow. Of course, if your testing-related business offers more limited services, or serves a very small or test-wary market, your income projections should be dialed back accordingly.

Every lab we spoke with, and several that have given investor talks and other public interviews, is profitable and growing. It's not a business for boot-strappers unless you have very big boots. But even that may be changing as micro labs offering simpler analysis of limited tests become more widely available.

Concentrate on concentrates

IF, AND ONLY IF:
- ✓   you have the necessary chemistry skills
- ✓   can afford to invest in substantial equipment costs
- ✓   are aware that your legal risks will be higher than most other marijuana industry businesses

then extraction of cannabis into various highly popular forms of **concentrates** may be the perfect super profitable business for you.

At recent industry business conferences, most recently in Las Vegas, extraction machinery and systems manufacturers have been very popular stops on most visitor's booth by booth walk of the exhibit hall. The technology is growing more affordable and no longer takes up a two car garage. But we are still super cautious about recommending this path to anyone who is not an accomplished professional in one of a couple of fields that will give you background to back up the training provided by the equipment company staff.

This is specialized equipment and you should move right along to the next potential idea for your business if you think it would be okay to brew up some hash oil in your apartment. This business opportunity is limited to folks with both start-up capital north of $50,000 and the necessary technical expertise, which may or may not be available through well-known training programs like Oaksterdam University, or more likely the extraction company themselves.

Extracts and concentrates are the super-potent outcome of large amounts of marijuana and some form of chemical, heat, cold, and/or Co2 extraction process, under pressure. Names for concentrates and extracts include hash oil, shatter, dabs, and a growing list of other slang and industry terms generally distinguished by the look and feel of the finished product.

We almost left concentrate and extraction businesses out of the book not because the start-up costs are high, or because concentrates are more legally controversial and risky in many places than other products, but because the risk of hurting yourself or others if you don't have proper equipment and training is high. More than any other type of business we've described, chemical processing of cannabis seems most likely to end you up on the evening news or in jail rather than running a happy, profitable business. Don't get us wrong: measured on profit potential, extraction of concentrated oils is likely to be phenomenally profitable. But you must not try to go home-brew, low-end. If you aren't confident that you can afford to follow the bed practices for safety...please don't do it. It's all fun and games until someone loses an eye.

How about starting a dispensary

IF YOUR DREAM BUSINESS IS a dispensary or other **retail marijuana business**, we have good news and bad news.

The good news is, that's a possibility.

The bad news is that retail cannabis businesses have much higher start-up costs, and heavier regulatory requirements, than virtually any other business you could choose to open. One medical marijuana advocate, discussing recent legalization and licensing discussions, said that it was easier to get licensed to open a distillery, a gun shop, and a brothel, than to open a legal medical marijuana business in most states. He might be exaggerating slightly about putting all 3 under one roof, but we did a quick search and the gun shops, at least, are far easier to open.

Those who do the meticulous leg work necessary to open a retail cannabusiness, regardless of what it is called in your chosen state, may also encounter rapidly escalating local regulations and taxes, less-than-supportive neighbors, and nervous landlords. So why does anyone do it?

Because there are great profits and huge levels of personal satisfaction available on the front lines of the medical, and now recreational, marijuana business. Helping patients/customers find the right combination of strains, delivery methods and dosage that eases whatever symptoms brought them through the door can be more rewarding than most people dream of finding their work.

Others in the retail business report great satisfaction in being part of the end of prohibition and have deeply personal commitments to helping make the legal retail industry all it can be.

Some dispensary and retail store owners simply see retail as the best use of their skills for the highest potential profit. One dispensary owner in Washington has been around marijuana for over twenty years, knows what patients want, and has the right contacts to provide high quality medication to his patient base. He also admits, to anyone who will listen, that he'd be a grower if it weren't for his black thumb. Dave says he can't keep a houseplant alive.

In short, there is a lot of investor capital to be raised and a lot of paper to push if your dream is a store that sells legal marijuana. Good luck, and write to tell us how the startup goes!

Hospitality innovation

SOME OF THE MOST ADVENTUROUS retailers are in the newly legal recreational markets and are feeling their way through both the regulatory thicket and trying to innovate to meet customer demand. The planned cannabis **smoking lounge**, with great infused food, and music that a partnership planned for Denver, was a bit too ahead of its time in 2014.

But the couple who spearheaded the project are committed trailblazers and have several other genuinely fresh ideas for serving the recreational market, within the legal framework, as it evolves. We share their excitement about future possibilities for expanding the margins of what retailers can provide in terms of recreational activities, combined entertainment or dining, and other hybrid models.

The first cannabis-friendly, and themed, **bed and breakfast inn** is already open and garnering rave reviews, in Colorado.

Your innovation may be another hospitality business that caters to the new class of cannabis tourists flooding into states with recreational legalization.

The Feds & Reefer Madness

THIS MAY BE A GOOD time to stop and point out that cannabis (marijuana, pot, weed, bud) is still labeled as a Schedule 1 drug by the United States government. This means that the federal government recognizes no legitimate use for marijuana and, when it feels like it, prosecutes people who sell, use, or grow marijuana— SEVERELY. Heroin is also a schedule 1 drug, to put the "no legitimate use" categorization and penalties in proper context.

Theoretically, businesses operating entirely legally under state law— with every permit, license, tax number, tagged plant, etc., in states with legal industries—could still run into raids, criminal investigations, financial or real estate seizures, and other super scary remedies available to the Drug Enforcement Administration (DEA).

The Justice Department has been saying since 2009 that prosecuting patients who use marijuana in compliance with state law "is unlikely to be an efficient use of limited federal resources." Unfortunately raids of some medical cannabis businesses, including the prosecution of 5 guys who were medical cannabis growers in rural Washington state, continue on an erratic basis.

As of this writing, December 2014, the IRS, due to a specific law passed by Congress to prevent criminals from deducting the tools of their trade, still does not allow deducting business expenses relating to legally-operated dispensaries or other legal, explicitly, cannabusinesses. Most entrepreneurs, and their legal and financial advisors, have divided their cannabis business from another non-cannibis related business—to make deducting legitimate business expenses legally possible.

In other words, the dispensary rent and utilities are definitely not deductible under federal tax code. The rest of the building you rent and use as a consulting practice, art studio, or café most certainly does have deductible expenses. Please, please don't mistake this for advice on legal or financial planning, or tax matters. Hire a canna-business specialist and set your business up right from the start.

My point here is only that government is moving toward setting up systems that ease legal cannabusinesses into a normal, tax-paying, bank-depositing NAICS category, if for no other reason than to make certain that each layer of government gets its share of the Grass Boom tax and licensure loot.

There is currently much debate about when and how the federal government will get out of the conflict set up with "free" medical marijuana states, by lowering or eliminating the scheduling of marijuana.

For now, you should take very seriously and comply to the nth degree with the obviously nutty treatment of the cannabis plant as a drug, including the prohibition on moving legally purchased cannabis across state lines.

- o   Never, ever mail cannabis product or proceeds. Mail fraud and related laws are hard federal time felonies. Don't do it. And no, FedEX is not an option. State lines are state lines.
- o   Pay every penny of local, state and federal tax you may

owe for any cannibis related business activities, in order to stay far, far away from the enforcement powers your federal government still has over marijuana.

○   Keep your non-cannabis related business and tax documents, returns, etc. in tip-top shape. This will help avoid being taxed at the no-deductions, cannabis penalty rate on your vintage Mustang parts eBay store, and also keep you clear of other accusations of under-reporting or under-payment.

○   Evaluate you and any business partners carefully when deciding whether you are a good fit for the high-scrutiny types of cannabusinesses such as grow operations and dispensaries. If you have an old felony for spitting on the wrong sidewalk in 1984, you need great legal advice on whether your place in the green rush should be in one of the higher-risk, higher-scrutiny service areas.

Real life example: Joan skinny-dipped in the town reservoir while a bit inebriated in 1993. She pled to indecent exposure and the judge waived the fine and everyone went their merry way. Fast forward to 2013. Joan now has been through three rounds of additional inquiries about her brush with youthful night-time nudity, and it looks like she, and her four business partners, will be turned down for a lucrative Washington state grow license—losing the thousands of dollars and hours their group spent preparing their business plan, gaining legal and other consulting etc. Joan didn't even remember the incident. Washington state computers remembered.

Huge amounts of legal, industry advocacy, financial investor, and political muscle are working to make it easier and more predictable to operate legal marijuana businesses. In the interval, be smart and careful out there. No-one wants to be made the example and get to wear orange for their trouble.

But for now, the federal threat does remain. There haven't been any high profile prosecutions of the new Colorado legal-marijuana entrepreneurs, but it could theoretically happen. There have been regular raids in California, and very recently in Colorado, of operations that the DEA and IRS said were operating far outside the legal requirements for legitimate marijuana grow and medical dispensary operations.

I'm not a federal judge, but I'm willing to bet a triple latte that the main "crime" of the busted businesses was sloppy or no record-keeping, and a failure to figure out a way to pay all local, state, and federal taxes that could possibly be due.

Some landlords, banks, crowd-funding sources, and investors are determined to stay on the sidelines of the Grass Rush, until the federal Schedule 1 problem is eliminated.

Maybe you should too. You will need to make your own decisions on your tolerance for risk. In our businesses, we handle no marijuana.

Marketing to Cannabusinesses

A NOTE HERE: MARIJUANA DISPENSARY owners and growers surveyed informally reported that their number one objection to vendor approaches and presentations was what they perceived as "price gouging." Vendors who saunter in thinking that price will be no object because "dispensaries and Boulder retailers are rolling in dough" will likely be shown the door.

Price your services reflecting the additional risks and costs of serving the emerging industry, and the likelihood that you will need to devote extra time to creating special systems etc. But do not abuse your new customer – you will price yourself right out of the market. Your reputation as a gouging vendor will precede you – news travels fast in the cannabis industry. Make the word-of-mouth underground work for you, not against you.

There is no better way to contact the hardworking folks who run medical marijuana cooperatives, collectives, and dispensaries, and recreational retail shops than to walk in during open hours, offer up a sample of your very best product, and then ask them for an order.

In many states, you'll need a patient card, or other documents indicating that you're eligible to buy or use medical marijuana, to get in the door. Appendix, How to Get Medical Marijuana, can help you thread that needle. If you're not already a patient or caregiver, you may find that it's worthwhile to learn about that status for better access to your market and pricing on any supplies you may need.

Since it is truly unlikely that you will be able to duplicate the walk-in strategy for all of your targeted customers, the next best thing is a call. Direct mail has also been successful for some vendors—if you prefer to send something in the mail, make sure you read about effective direct mail before you spend any postage.

The list of dispensaries is provided as a starting point to your edibles business marketing efforts. Once you've contacted a few dispensaries, described what your company offers, and asked whether they would be interested in discussing your service or sampling your products, you'll have a great start on a successful marketing plan.

This will be true whether your first conversations lead to immediate orders or result in questions, suggestions, or even a request that you call back at a slower time in their day.

Look at these calls as a learning process rather than as sales calls. The difference between success and failure, in every business we've ever run, is in whether you are willing to make the exploratory calls to your target market. You won't run out of dispensaries so don't worry if your presentation is awkward or shy, at first. Make your calls and the orders will follow.

Here is a simple script to get you started:

"Hi, This is Annie at Annie's Incredible Edibles, may I ask if your dispensary carries edibles? (Yes, no, sometimes, we used to).

Great. Are you finding a growing demand for edibles? (Great, or I see.)

Annies is dedicated to providing dispensaries with a reliable supply of the best edibles available.

Should I send you a sample, or does someone else at Medical Mary Jane Miracles, handle the edibles selection?"

Listen. Take notes. Refine your message based on responses. Confirm names and mailing addresses so that you can follow up accurately.

No complete dispensary or retailer list for legal cannabis exists. The current reality of the state-specific legalization wave is that being in the marijuana business often involves moving with changes to local zoning or other rules, expanding product lines or license type, adding delivery only service areas, etc. Also, new dispensaries open every day...great news for your service or product (the market is growing) but tough to keep up to date in a book. So each state broken out below has links to online resources that can help you find your clients.

There are some good sources of dispensary and retail store information on the internet. Weed Maps (weedmaps.com) is probably the best known but we also like theWeedBlog.com. Leafly.com is another option.

Naming your business

I'M GOING OUT ON A limb here because some of my favorite people run successful cannabusinesses with catchy in-crowd names...but if you're considering entering the legal marijuana industry at any level, branding starts with your name, and you need to know the scoop on it.

LadyBud is a super online publication that is "Classing up the joint." 420 this and MJ that makes a statement...to the in-crowd. MJ Freeway is a wink and a nod to Mary Jane slang and an industry software leader, but none of these slang references mean anything to many newcomers to the industry. I can usually tell whether someone is a newbie by whether they ask me if my name, Megan Deal, is my 'real name.'

High Times is High Times. But you may do better with Anderson Dispensary Bookkeeping Services. Child-proof Packaging Pros, or Vape News. The more the industry matures, the less cute and catchy names will help you rise to the top of the class.

I freely admit that I am biased toward a bit more seriousness: Marijuana Business Tax Services is far more appealing than Mary Jane's Smokin Tax Service. Dispensary Tax Experts, LLC does an even better job of saying what you do without giving an unintentional teenage stoner vibe to your business. Dispensary

Cleaning Services, LLC, lets your potential customers know exactly what you offer without a hint of the immature slang that undermines your professional image.

Your mileage may vary but with every passing industry meeting and trade show, we are happy to see fewer and fewer slang-named businesses. Maybe it's because so many of us who are involved in the growth of the legalized marijuana industry are (ahem) older, and either never partook of marijuana culture as younger folks, or at the very least haven't seen a copy of High Times or a joint in decades, but a name that says what you do in plain language might be your best bet to reach the widest market. Don't make us use a glossary to get the in-crowd reference in your business name.

An exception to this branding advice may be cases where you are targeting your business directly to cannabis consumers. If you sell a magazine at 420 festivals, or glassware at craft fairs, feel free to go with a name worthy of a Grateful Dead concert.

Here, our focus is primarily on businesses that are providing services and products on a business to business basis and even the hippest edible or t-shirt companies may find that in 2015, retailers would rather pay an invoice with a well thought-out, professional business brand name at the top.

One further thought on this branding topic: Current cannabis businesses are often quite focused on attracting investors, and the stability and and legitimacy that successful 'angel' and similar investor groups can lend to cannabusiness brands. Investors I know, and their bankers, do not generally embrace the big green leaf logo with the slang/catch phrase name. Picture your business name on the Profit & Loss or vendor profile for your prospective customer—and decide for yourself whether it passes the investor comfort zone test.

Of course, you'll want your prospective customers to know that you are supportive of the post-prohibition marijuana industry and it is great to put that support out there, loud and clear, in your marketing materials. You can also signal your loyalty and interest by joining and actively supporting appropriate business associations and events. "Serving the California medical marijuana industry with quality payroll services since 2013" makes the point.

More and more marijuana-based businesses are seeking out mainstream firms to help them transition into the fully regulated and legal era. Your firm, whether a brand new start-up or an established business, can help make the marijuana marketplace more professional while providing you the opportunity to build profits only available in markets that are undergoing the kind of rapid growth and change that offers such a great opportunity to those of us ready to jump into the legal marijuana industry now.

Medical Marijuana: 23 states of cannabis legality

So you don't live in Colorado, Washington, Oregon or Alaska? Good news: you can still get your share of the legalization boom. Medical access to marijuana is available in 23 states.

There is a LOT of variation among them as to how 'medical access' is defined. Among the questions about your state's access laws are:

What disease, disorder or condition does the patient need to document?

How many doctors, and which ones, can document?

What specific marijuana products are legalized?

Who can produce those products? and of course

How can patients get access to 'medical marijuana'—who gets to sell it?

As you can see, the business opportunities in your state or local area may be amplified or constricted based on how these questions are answered.

For example: If you live in a state that allows or requires licensed retailers, called 'dispensaries', to sell 'medical use' marijuana, those dispensaries have service requirements for what they can sell, to whom, for how much, how they collect and pay taxes on the transactions, and whether the neighbors have to know/can't find out about their dispensary location. Each of these items represents a business service opportunity for you, in:

✓ Product development and manufacture
✓ Patient paperwork auditing
✓ Accounting and tax prep
✓ Signage
✓ Real estate

Because regulation varies around the US, you need to know the rules for your state.

Washington

WASHINGTON

DISPENSARIES

SEATAC AREA

8TH Wonder   11220 Pacific Ave S Tacoma, WA 98444
   253 314 5103

A Green Cure   910 N 145th St Shoreline, WA 98133
   206 466 1264

A Greener Today   9509 Rainier Ave S Seattle, WA 98118
   206 257 0894

Advanced Healing 17512 66th Ave Court E Puyallup, WA 98375
   253 507 4652

All Natural Wellness Collective
   816 72nd St E Tacoma, WA 98404
   253 314 5340

Altercare   828 Rainier Ave S Seattle, WA 98144
   206 329 2223

Alternative Care Clinic   5609 4th Ave S Seattle, WA 98108
   206 629 2122

Amazing Gardens 517 Central Ave S Kent, WA 98032
   253 850 7688

Ancient Holistic Remedies   4040 S Tyler St Suite 7 Tacoma, WA 98409   253 304 0957

Ancient Medicine Collective   3716 Pacific Ave Suite G Tacoma, WA 98418 253 383 3507

Belltown Community Gardens Seattle
    2224 2nd Ave Seattle, WA 98121
    206 728 4053

Bloom Room Tacoma   5225 South Tacoma Way Tacoma, WA 98409   253 448 2146

Brave Hearts 7046 Pacific Ave Tacoma, WA 98408
    253 302 4192

Brave Hearts Delivery   Delivery Only
    253 302 4192

Bud Lady   Delivery Only   206 601 0506

Canapa 5432 S Tacoma Way Tacoma, WA 98409
    253 212 3856

Canna Club   6223 112th St E Puyallup, WA 98373
    253 256 4223

Canna Rx   3601 Fremont Ave N Ste 210 Seattle, WA 98103
    206 588 1637

Cannabis Club Collective   2706 6th Ave North Tacoma, WA 98406   253 507 4725

Cannabis Emporium   5324 84th St E Tacoma, WA 98446
    253 292 0821

CannaPi   6111 12th Ave S South Seattle, WA 98108
    206 763 1171

Cannatonics Society   711 Opera Alley Court C Tacoma, WA 98402   253 302 5539

Center Street Collective 4915 Center Street Suite D Tacoma, WA 98409   253 564 1108

Cesar's Salad3908 Aurora Ave N Seattle, WA 98103

206 547 5754

Chronic Solutions Co-op   136 Stewart Rd SE Suite 1E Pacific, WA 98047 253 447 7480

Clear Choice Collective 8001 So Hosmer St Tacoma, WA 98408
253 444 5444

Cloners Market   11740 Aurora Ave N Seattle, WA 98133
206 792 9910

Cloneville Seattle 9258 57th Ave S Seattle, WA 98118
206 725 7092

Conscious Care Cooperative – Ballard
1701 NW Market Street Seattle, WA 98107
206 297 6043

Conscious Care Cooperative – North Seattle
8554 Greenwood Ave N Seattle, WA 98103
206 789 1492

Conscious Care Cooperative of Lake
8288 Lake City Way NE Seattle, WA 98115
206 829 9909

Conscious Care Cooperative of North Seattle
14032 Aurora Ave N Suite C North Seattle, WA 98133
206 466 1206

Conscious Care Delivery of South King County
Delivery Only   206 250 5969

Cool, Calm, Collective   12309 15th Ave NE Suite B Seattle, WA 98125   206 365 5737

Covington Holistic Dr. Vape   16204 SE 272nd St Covington, WA 98042   253 630 3050

Cure Collective   12110 Meridian E Suite #3 Puyallup, WA 98373
253 604 4607

Cut Loose Collective   8601 14th Ave S South Seattle, WA 98108
206 588 0744

Dab City   3320 Rainier Ave South Seattle, WA 98144
253 670 3669

Delightful Caregivers   4421 Rainier Ave S Seattle, WA 98118
425 829 8502

Delta 9 Seattle   1950 1st Ave S Seattle, WA 98134
206 525 4202

Dockside Co-op   223 N 36th St Seattle Central, WA 98013
206 420 4837

Eastside Free Delivery   Delivery Only
206 735 1294

Eastside Greenlight   230 NE Juniper St #100 Issaquah, WA
98027   425 391 1500

Eastside Herbal Care   Delivery Only
425 260 4150

Eastside Organics Delivery Only
425 531 2491

Emerald City Collective Gardens
3161 Elliot Ave Suite 102 Downtown Seattle, WA 98121
206 462 1050

Emerald Pharms   3805 45th Street Tacoma, WA 98409
253 475 2100

Evergreen Bud And Glass   1956 1st Ave South Seattle, WA
98134   206 623 3792

Evergreen Medical Gardens   32201 Kent/Black Diamond Rd
Auburn, WA 98092   253 737 5659

Evergreen Medicinal Gardens 2907 72nd St E Tacoma, WA 98404
253 327 1214

Everyday Essentials   7824 River Road E Suite E Puyallup, WA
98371   253 446 6443

Farmacy   102 South Military Road Suite B Tacoma, WA 98444
253 539 3276

Fire House   3852 S Center St Tacoma, WA 98409
   253 267 0715
Firefly   Delivery Only   360 607 5213
Fremont Gardens 316 North 36th St Seattle, WA 98102
   206 632 7126
Fweedom Collective   12001 Aurora Ave N Seattle, WA 98133
   206 734 9333
GNU Organics   9988 15th Ave SW Suite G Seattle, WA 98146
   206 697 6482
Green Aid   Delivery Only   206 743 2864
Green Ambrosia – King County
   Delivery Only   206 496 2345
Green Ambrosia Wellness Center
   7730 15th Ave NW Seattle, WA 98117
   206 496 2345
Green Anne @ Queen Anne   312 W Republican St Seattle, WA
98119   206 420 1042
   Green Cafe Collective   13417 Pacific Ave Tacoma, WA 98444
   253 302 4106
   Green Collar Club 10422 Pacific Ave S Suite B Tacoma, WA 98444
   253 267 0675
   Green Door Seattle   1207 S Jackson St Ste 109 South Seattle,
Washington 98144   206 618 7133
   Green Magic Collection 5303 Rainier Ave S Suite D Seattle, WA
98118   206 453 3623
   Green Monster Club   5105 N 46th St Tacoma, WA 98407
   253 241 2948
   Green Skunk 11231 Roosevelt Way NE Seattle, WA 98125
   206 417 1973
   Green Solution   15941 Meridian East Puyallup, WA 98375
   253 845 0525

Greenhand   3107 Eastlake Ave E Seattle, WA 98102
206 735 7072

GreenHealth Cooperative   5307 4th Ave S South Seattle, WA
98108   206 730 0979

GreenLink Collective   160 NW Gilman Blvd Suite I Issquah, WA
98027   425 677 7446

GreenLink Collective SODO   2224 1st ave Seattle, WA 98134
206 402 6353

Greenside Medical 9804 Lake City Way NE North Seattle, WA
98115   206 380 3129

Greenworks Cooperative   11064 Lake City Way NE #6 North
Seattle, WA 98125   206 922 3911

Have A Heart Cafe 4500 9th Ave NE Seattle, WA 98105
206 708 7443

Have A Heart CC   11736 Aurora Ave N North Seattle, WA 98133
206 257 4500

Herbal Choice Caregivers   19011 68th Ave S Ste A-110 Kent,
WA 98032 253 981 4444

Herbal Collective   6204 112th Street E Puyallup, WA 98373
253 256 4251

Herbal Gardens   824 South 28th Street Tacoma, WA 98409
253 272 5265

Herbal Generation 16804 Pacific Ave S Suite B Spanaway, WA
98387   253 212 9197

Herbal Health CC   5303 Rainier Ave S Suite E Seattle, WA 98118
206 453 4960

Herbal Health Center Inc Collective
5520 112th St E Suite B1 Puyallup, WA 98373
253 845 5480

Herbal Market Boutique 10422 16th Ave SW Seattle, WA 98146
206 397 4929

Herban Legends   9619 16th Ave SW South Seattle, WA 98106
206 849 5596
House Of Cannabis   217 174th St S Spanaway, WA 98387
253 537 0444
IgreenLife   Delivery Only   206 687 5023
Integrity Care Delivery   Delivery Only
206 499 5291
Joint Cooperative 5265 University Way Seattle Central, WA 98105
206 283 3333
Kured Collective Delivery Service
Delivery Only   1 855 87 KURED
Lady Buds   31515 3rd Ave Black Diamond, WA 98010
360 469 4143
Left Coast Cannabis   7604 South Tacoma Way Ste B Tacoma,
WA 98409 800 877 5785
Life Tree   12409 Renton Ave S South Seattle, WA 98178
206 683 0508
Lifes Rx – Renton 3904 NE 4th St #103 Renton, WA 98056
425 572 5905
Lucky Ladyz 2628 Alki Ave SW Seattle, WA 98116
206 466 5144
MAP   South Lake Union Seattle, WA 98109
206 682 2545
Mary Jane Gardens   8733 Greenwood Ave N Seattle, WA
98103   206 457 8319
MedCan Delivery   Delivery Only
206 728 7711
MediGreen Access Point   11012 Canyond Rd E Suite 43
Puyallup, WA 98373 253 531 3192
Midland Alternative Care   8614 Portland Ave E Unit C Tacoma,
WA 98445 253 301 0619

MMJ Universe Farmers Market
26130 SE Green Valley Rd Black Diamond, WA 98010
253 315 2673
Mountain Leaf Collective   19815 Mountain Hwy E Spanaway,
WA 98387 253 666 3305
Mountain Medicine Clinic   10217 128th St E Ste E Puyallup, WA
98374   253 256 4015
Natural Care 2309 Tacoma Ave S Tacoma, WA 98402
253 214 6983
Natural Care 2   3028 River Road E Tacoma, WA 98443
253 922 5687
Natural Green Medicine 4701 Roosevelt Way NE Suite B Seattle,
WA 98105 206 557 4632
Natural Therapy Collective   18407 Pacific Ave Suite 1 Spanaway,
WA 98387 253 271 0121
Naturally Green Access Point 10821 Valley East Puyallup, WA
98372   253 256 4007
Natures Resource Center   3833 Pacific Ave Suite C N Tacoma,
WA 98418 253 572 5544
New Millennium   14040 Aurora Ave North Seattle, WA 98133
206 466 2029
New Millennium   3867 Rainier Ave S Seattle, WA 98118
206 725 8451
Nice Guys   11457 Pacific Ave Suite 8 Tacoma, WA 98444
253 531 8051
No Worries Deliveries   Delivery Only
206 631 0511
North Seattle Med Co   Delivery Only
206 462 5353
NorthWest Best Alternative Medicine
4534 South Pine Street Tacoma, WA 98409

253 627 0248

Northwest Cannabis Market   9640 16th Ave SW South Seattle, WA 98106   206 420 4823

Northwest Cannabis Market Galaxy
2329 Rainier Ave Seattle, WA 98144
206 420 4065

Northwest Evergreen Garden 510 ½ 112th St Tacoma, WA 98444
253 503 3132

Northwest Kush Collective   135 NW 85th St Seattle, WA 98117
206 420 4917

Northwest Patient Resource Center
1809 Minor Avenue #101 Seattle, WA 98101
206 623 0848

Northwest Patient Resource Center
9456 35th Avenue SW Seattle, WA 98126
206 588 2841

One Love Collective   Delivery Only
206 227 8088

Oven Mitt   1625 E 72nd St Ste 700-215 Tacoma, WA 98404
206 856 6375

Pacific Coast Natural Medicine
9817 16th Ave SW Seattle, WA 98106
206 851 0849

Pacific Green And Delivery   136 Stewart Rd SE Suite 1G Pacific, WA 98046 206 395 6351

Pacific Green And Delivery   1202 A Street South East Auburn, WA 98002 206 395 6351

Patient Care Network   921 S Harney St Seattle, WA 98108
206 397 4197

Patient Resource Group Delivery Only
253 208 7724

PDA Lounge 2224 2nd Ave Seattle, WA 98121
206 728 4053

Pharmaseed Delivery Only   206 369 3452

Plump   2258 15th Ave W Seattle, WA 98119
206 765 7289

Power Plant Health   10217 123rd St Ct E Puyallup, WA 98374
253 268 0947

Professional Patient Co-op   1421 N 34th St Suite A Seattle, WA
98103   206 402 6643

Pugent Sound Health Alternatives
3202 15th Ave West Seattle Central, WA 98119
206 402 5082

Queen Anne Cannabis Club   533 1st Ave West Seattle, WA 98119
206 282 2441

Rain City Magnolia   2112 Thorndyke Ave W Seattle, WA 98199
206 659 4303

Rain City Medical   11537 Rainier Ave S Seattle, WA 98178
206 772 0023

Rainier Wellness Center 3111 S Pine St Tacoma, WA 98409
253 302 3365

Royal Green Medical   5205 S Tacoma, WA 98409
253 282 1833

Safe Access   3809 Delridge Way SW Seattle, WA 98106
206 466 5678

Seashore Collective   17517 15th Ave NE Shoreline, WA 98155
206 687 7787

Seattle Green Light CC 9211 Delridge Way South West Seattle,
WA 98106 206 497 MEDS

Seattle Medical Marijuana Association
4465 Fremont Ave N Seattle, WA 98103
206 883 0573

Seattle Quality Collective   13760 Aurora Ave North Seattle, WA 98133   206 257 4941

SMC Tacoma 8236 Pacific Ave S Tacoma, WA 98408
   253 472 0192

Smoke Time 18820 Aurora Ave N #206 Shoreline, WA 98133
   206 629 5642

Sodo Holistic Health   3232 1st Ave S Seattle, WA 98134
   206 257 5074

Solution   14343 15th Ave NE Seattle, WA 98125
   206 364 1226

Solution   8600 Lake City Way NE Seattle, WA 98115
   206 306 6968

Sound Remedies Mix And Match
   13507 Meridian Ave Ste M Puyallup, WA 98373
   253 268 0224

Source 118 S Washington St Seattle Central, WA 98104
   206 395 2036

South King Holistic   2824 S 252nd St Kent, WA 98032
   253 854 5900

South Sound Holistic Medicine
   21110 Meridian E #A Graham, WA 98338
   253 271 0017

Stash Box   2701 N 21st St Tacoma, WA 98406
   253 625 7905

Steele Green Collective Garden
   11401 Steele St South Tacoma, WA 98444
   253 539 9057

Summit Group Collective   1215 Earnest S Brazill St Tacoma, WA 98405 253 627 1845

Sun Can Delivery Delivery Only
   206 535 7645

Sweet Herbal Co-op   3847 Rainier Ave S Ste #5 Seattle, WA 98118   206 760 6105

T-Town Alternative Medicine 4823 S 66th Street Tacoma, WA 98408   253 226 5973

Tacoma Holistic Collective   3908 6th Ave Ste B Tacoma, WA 98406   253 292 0591

Tacoma Way 2607 S Tacoma Way Tacoma, WA 98409
253 292 0835

The Kind Alternative Medical 30355 SE High Point Way Preston, WA 98050 425 222 3909

The Solution 13955 SE 173rd Place Renton, WA 98058
253 239 2789

TIN Collective   4502 S Union Ave Tacoma, WA 98409
253 426 1289

Top Choice Wellness Center Renton
19861 Renton Maple Valley Road South East Maple Valley, WA 98038   206 491 3582

Tranquility Holistic Center   911 S 3rd St Renton, WA 98057
425 207 8504

Trees Collective   10532 Greenwood Ave N Seattle, WA 98133
206 257 4407

Tribal Collective Garden   1637 E 72nd St Tacoma, WA 98404
253 306 2842

Urban Healing Collective   Delivery Only
206 747 2495

WCC   9809 16th Ave SW Suite C Seattle, WA 98106
206 432 9204

White Center Alternative Care
9839 17th Ave SW Seattle, WA 98106
206 743 8385

Woodinville Alternative Medicine

21127 State Route 9 Woodinville WA 98072

425 415 3800

Woodinville Quality Collective

23128 State Route 9 SE #2 Woodinville, WA 98072

425 402 9647

Kitsap County

Big Buddas Collective Meds   4231 Olympic Dr Bremerton, WA 98312   360 265 0236

Cannabis Care Foundation   23150 NE State Route 3 Belfair, WA 98528   360 552 2420

Care-med Co-op 12402 134th Ave kpn Gig Harbor, WA 98329   253 857 2288

Dreamweaver Growers   Delivery Only
   360 598 1880

Emerald Coast Collective   1600 NW Roseway Inn #100 Bremerton, WA 98311   360 813 1006

Evergreen Health Center   1405 NE McWilliams Rd Suite 103 Bremerton, WA 98311   360 377 0192

Green Comfort   3280 SE Lund Port Orchard, WA 98366
   360 519 3753

Greenthumb Port Orchard   4978 Mile Hill Dr Port Orchard, WA 98366   360 443 2293

Greenthumb Silverdale 2839 NW Kitsap Place #A Silverdale WA 98383   360 698 0353

Harbor Alternative Wellness 6708 144th NW Suite A Gig Harbor, WA 98332 253 514 8374

Herbal Healing Collective Garden
   3062 SW Hwy 16 Suite A Port Orchard, WA 98367
   360 813 3644

Kitsap Cannabis Farmers Fair 4211 Feigley Rd W Bremerton, WA

98312   360 519 4274

KP Healing Center 9507 State Route 302 Gig Harbor, WA 98329
253 858 6375

KPN Quality Collective   15607 92nd Street Lake Bay, WA 98349
253 884 6420

Mari Meds   23710 NE State Route 3 Belfair, WA 98528
360 275 1181

Top Green Meds   2135 Sheridan Rd Suite D Bremerton, WA
98310   360 479 9172

Vancouver Area

Clear Mind Medical   Delivery Only
360 448 5296

Eagle's Nest Cannabis Delivery
Delivery Only   360 773 6213

Firefly   Delivery Only   360 607 5213

Fullys Wildflower   Delivery Only
360 953 0771

Grass Rootz 1411 West Side Hwy Kelso, WA 98626
360 353 3035

Green Cross Delivery Only   360 574 5544

Marandas   4503 Ocean Beach Longview, WA 98632
360 577 0800

Medi Brothers Collective   Delivery Only
360 258 0764

Olympia

Canatopia Too   2747 Pacific Ave SE Olympia, WA 98501
360 350 0984

Earth Alternative Medicine   1123 Sleater kinney Rd SE Suite A
Lacey, WA 98503   360 688 7395

Evergreen Alternative Medicine
2716 Pacific Ave Olympia, WA 98501
360 915 8992
Firefly   Delivery Only   206 303 7851
Green Acres 420   2625 Martin Way East Olympia, WA 98597
360 350 0891
Green Meds   Delivery Only   360 561 9955
Healthy Element   430 Carpenter Road SE Suite A Lacey WA
98503   360 556 7247
Hybrid 360 Farms 6311 Rich Rd SE Olympia, WA 98501
360 438 2060
Mari Meds Too   3811 State Route 3 Shelton, WA 98584
360 426 0420
Medical Caregivers Collective Gardens
304 East Pine St Oakville, WA 98568
360 858 7270
Mud Bay Meds   5021 Mud Bay Rd NW Olympia, WA 98502
360 878 8754
Natural 7   6020 Pacific Ave SE Ste M Lacey, WA 98503
360 489 1308
NorthWest Alternative Care   2210 Black Lake Blvd SW Suite G1
Olympia, WA 98512 360 352 1242
Northwest Alternative Collective Care
1800 Cooper Point Rd SW Bldg #2 Olympia, WA 98512
360 688 1114
NW Express   234 Division St Olympia, WA 98502
360 943 9338
Olympia Alternative Medicine
2405 Harrison Ave NW Olympia, WA 98502
360 705 9415
Olympic Medical Group 1965 4th Ave E Olympia, WA 98506

360 338 0986

Ranier Xpress   117 Legion Way SW Olympia, WA 98501
   360 489 0132

Serious Medicine Collective   322 4th Ave Olympia, WA 98502
   360 943 9658

Urban Medicinals 121 Legion Way SW Olympia, WA 98501
   360 915 7102

Olympic Peninsula Area

Firefly Delivery Only   206 303 7851

HoodCanal Patient2Patient Co-op
   22090 N US Hwy 101 Potlach, WA 98548
   360 877 2700

Karma Wellness Cooperative 2839 Hwy 101 E Port Angeles, WA
98362   360 504 1115

Medical Express   Delivery Only
   360 461 9089

Olympic Organics Delivery Only
   360 419 5567

Tantra Herbal Care And Wellness
   2807 Olympic Hwy Aberdeen, WA 98520
   360 637 9421

Bellingham Area

Ferntucky Medical 5982 Portal Way Ferndale, WA 98248
   360 550 5669

Green Piece 17910 State Route 536 Suite A Mt Vernon, WA
98273   360 982 2290

Healthy Living Center   4140 Meridian St Suite 220 Bellingham,
WA 98225 360 778 3904

Kind Green Botanicals Collective

1311 11th St Bellingham, WA 98225
360 671 5991
Samish Way Holistic Center   1326 E Laurel St Bellingham, WA
98225   360 733 3838
Skagit Valley Collective 20291 Hwy 20, Burlington, WA 98284
360 707 2801
True Health Care   6920 A2 Guide Meridian Rd Lynden, WA 98264
360 656 5983
True Holistic Care Delivery Only
360 483 6803

Everett Area
221 Rx 18729 Fir Island Rd Suite C Conway, WA 98238
360 445 4221
A Green Cure Snohomish   8501 168th St SE Suite C
Snohomish, WA 98296   360 863 3529
Ahh Yes Cannabis Delivery Only
855 360 BUDS
Chubby Pig   Delivery Only   360 547 9043
Conscious Care Delivery   Delivery Only
425 610 0750
Evergreen Patient Network   2520 Center Rd Ste A Everett, WA
98204   425 299 0377
Green Rush Collective   14608 Hwy 99 Suite 304 Lynnwood, WA
98087   425 678 8106
Harlee Cooperative   14031 52nd Ave W Edmonds, WA 98026
360 393 9064
Healing Leaf Collective Garden
9626 32nd St Se Lake Stevens, WA 98258
425 322 5273
High Caliber Medical Group 8920 84th ST NE Arlington, WA

98223   360 547 2680

HypeHerbally Holistic Health 1120 112th St SW Everett, WA 98204
425 280 9482

Joint Co-op 16510 State Route 9 SE Snohomish, WA 98296
360 243 3399

Med Source Patient Network 15315 Hwy 99 Lynwood, WA 98087
425 743 7704

MedCan Delivery   Delivery Only
206 321 9496

Medical Marijuana Patients   4204 Russell Rd Suite A Mukilteo,
WA 98275 425 346 4533

Patient2Patient   8004 Mukliteo Speedway Mukliteo, WA 98275
425 249 2047

Riverside Wellness Center   8411 SR 92 Suite 2 Granite Falls, WA
98252   360 322 7257

Spokane Area

Alternative MMD Co-op 1506 N Pines Spokane Valley, WA 99206
509 475 0723

CCCMMP   Delivery Only   509 842 2877

Cool Calm Collective Delivery
Delivery Only   206 457 6097

Direct Medical   Delivery Only
509 262 4519

Dr Green Thumbs 122 N University Suite 200 Spokane Valley, WA
99206   509 808 5080

Herbal Connection Inc 3812 N Monroe St Spokane, WA 99205
509 315 8459

High Society Delivery Only   509 413 8057

JD's Collective Garden   39817 N Newport Hwy Elk, WA 99009
509 292 0439

Lilac City Collective Association
  1716 N Ash St Spokane, WA 99205
  509 262 6413
Northside Alternative Wellness Center
  4811 N Market Spokane, WA 99217
  509 241 3306
PNWM   805 E Houston Ave Spokane, WA 99208
  509 474 9275
Simple Confidential Ideal   Delivery Only
  509 209 8621
Spocannabis 120 E Mission Ave Spokane, WA 99202
  509 998 3405
Spot Collective Garden Inc   3625 E Ferry Ave Spokane, WA
99202   509 534 0476

Pullman Area
Cool Calm Collective Delivery
  Delivery Only   509 496 7213
Herb Delight Delivery Only   509 910 7253

Oregon

Oregon Dispensaries

Portland Area

Alberta Organics   1207 NE Alberta St Portland, OR 97211
   503 206 4781

Alternative Farmacy/Happiness
   10340 NE Weidler St Portland, OR 97220
   503 255 0092

Alternative Remedies   6031 SE Foster Rd Portland, OR 97206
   971 279 5243

Alternative Solutions   13560 SE Powell Blvd Portland, OR 97236
   503 761 1635

Alternative Wellness Center   5241 SE 72nd Ave Portland, OR
97206   971 888 4392

Brightside   1010 SE Powell Blvd Portland, OR 97202
   503 206 8726

Brothers Cannabis Club 3609 SE Division Street Portland, OR
97202   503 894 8001

Buddha's Bliss   Delivery Service
   360 450 9712

Cannabis Outreach Collective

Delivery Service 503 853 1319
Cannabliss – Portland   1917 SE 7th Ave Portland, OR 97214
  503 719 4338
Cascade Alternative Resources
  6430 NE MLK Blvd Portland, OR 97211
  503 284 6714
Clean Cut Clones Delivery Service
  503 277 3635
Club Sky High   8957 N Lombard St Portland, OR 97203
  503 719 5801
Collective Awakenings 2823 NE Sandy Blvd Portland, OR 97232
  503 206 7090
Doy's West Side Home Delivery
  Delivery Service 503 597 9221
Eagle's Nest – Cannabis Specialists
  Delivery Service 360 773 6213
Eco Firma Farms – Wholesale Garden
  2239 NE Broadway Portland, OR 97232
  971 276 6100
Eden   1155 SE 82nd St Portland, OR 97216
  971 271 3825
Emerald Rose City Cannabis Club
  17030 SE McLoughlin Blvd Portland, OR 97267
  503 654 7104
Farmacy   19151 SE Burnside Gresham, OR 97030
  503 489 5502
Flower To The People   7540 NE Sandy Blvd Portland, OR 97213
  503 706 7770
Franks Collective 7112 NE Glisan St Portland, OR 97213
  503 256 6869
Freedom Pharmacy   11905 NE Halsey Portland, OR 97230

971 888 5909

Gr8 Stop Med Shop   4844 A NE 103rd Portland, OR 97220
971 279 4178

Grass And Glass Hopper LLC Delivery Service
971 221 0954

Great Ape Collective   9053 NE Sandy Blvd #A Portland, OR 97220   971 255 0317

Green Haus   3706 SE Powell Blvd Portland, OR 97202
503 232 1122

Green Karma Delivery   Delivery Service
360 356 6041

Green Remedy   12447 SE Powell Blvd Portland, OR 97236
503 761 0226

Grower Patient Resources   3205 SE 13th Ave Suite 420 Portland, OR 97202   503 236 4204

Harvest Connoisseur   Delivery Service
971 231 4842

Hashford Club   8001 SE 72nd Ave Portland, OR 97206
503 477 8106

Herb Collection   4603 SE Hawthorne Blvd Portland, OR 97215
503 239 7777

Herbalist Farmer   45 NE 122 Ave Portland, OR 97220
503 252 9088

Holistic Remedies 4730 North Lombard Street Portland, OR 97203   503 894 8946

Human Collective II   9220 SW Barbur Blvd Suite 106 Portland, OR 97219 503 208 3042

Lewis And Clark Collective   16955 SE Division St Portland, OR 97236   971 279 4932

Local Herb Collective   15948 SE Division St Portland, OR 97236
503 433 8030

Maritime Cafe   17415 SE McLoughlin Blvd Gladstone OR 97267   503 305 8307

Mt Hood Wellness Center   14325 SE Stark St Portland, OR 97233   971 279 4116

Multnomah Wellness   818 SW 1st Ave Portland, OR 97204
   503 241 2808

Natural Alternatives Delivery Delivery Service
   503 616 6604

Northern Lighterz Holistic Co-op
   3200 N Lombard Portland, OR 97217
   503 283 7600

Northwest Health Center LLC 6126 SE Duke St Unit A Portland, OR 97206   503 851 9709

NWRC/Portside Patient Services
   8937 N Lombard Street Portland, OR 97203
   971 279 4130

Oregon Medical Cannabis University
   2900 SW Cornelius Pass Rd. Suite 547 & 548 Hillsboro, OR 97123   503 649 2999

OMMC 3500 NE 82nd Ave Portland, OR 97220
   971-302-6993

OMMC 10055 SE Glisan St Portland, OR 97220
   503-716-6042

OMMP Resource Center 1310 SE 7th Ave Portland, OR 97214
   971 255 1456

Oregon Cannabis High Society
   Delivery Service 503 419 7888

PDX Natural Access   3022 E Burnside St Portland, OR 97214
   971 271 8048

PK Delivery   Delivery Service 971 258 7027

Portland Canna Connection   1515 SE 46th Ave Portland, OR

97215   503 477 9247
Portland Compassionate Caregivers
4020 SE Cesar E Chavez Blvd Portland, OR 97239
503 954 2275
Portland Medical Cannabis Club
4611 Southwest Beaverton-Hillsdale Hwy Portland, OR 97221
971 279 5370
Portland Patient Resource Collective
110 SE Main #C Portland, OR 97214
503 477 4261
Portland's Best Meds Delivery Service
Delivery Service 503 616 3852
POTlandia   7131 NE Prescott Portland, OR 97218
503 719 7214
Power Plant   Delivery Service 503 875 9336
Pure Oregon 2410 N Mississippi Portland, OR 97227
503 954 3902
ReLeaf MM   Delivery Service 360 773 8810
Releaf Portland Delivers 1034 SE 122nd Ave Portland, OR 97233
503 278 9237
Rip City Remedies 3325 SE Division St Portland, OR 97206
503 235 6000
Rose City Oreganics   5134 SE Foster Portland, OR 97206
503 788 3351
Rose City Wellness Center   3821 NE Martin Luther King Blvd
Portland, OR 97212 503 384 2251
Rosebud Wellness Center   2239 NE Broadway Portland, OR
97232   503 432 8937
StumpTown Theraputics   Delivery Service
503 252 9403
Sweet Leaf Illusions   8434 SE 82nd Ave Portland, OR 97266

503 719 5322
Top Flight Delivery PDX Delivery Service
503 915 8992
TreeHouse Collective   2915 NE Broadway St Unit C Portland, OR 97232   503 894 8774
Urban Collective   305 NW 21st Ave Suite 200 Portland, OR 97209
503 895 8551
Veterans Alternative Resource Center
9103 SW Barbur Blvd Portland, OR 97219
503 245 5546
World Famous Cannabis Cafe
322 SE 82nd Ave Portland, OR 97216
503 208 3395

Salem Area
1st Choice Cannabis   4142 Liberty Rd South Salem, OR 97306
971 301 0744
CannaMedicine Co-op 1527 State St Salem, OR 97301
971 240 1777
Cherry City Compassion   2025 25th St SE Salem, OR 97302
971 273 7607
Club Pitbull   4088 State St Salem, OR 97301
503 409 8192
Herbal Remedies   1729 Center St NE Suite 170 Salem, OR 97301
503 584 1755
Holistic Choice   1045 Commercial Street SE Salem, OR 97302
503 990 7312
Oregon Chronic Solutions   2615 Silverton Rd NE Salem, OR 97301   503 385 8101
Top Shelf LLC   2350 State St Salem, OR 97301
503 990 6723

Eugene
OMMP Farmers Market
730 W 7th Ave Eugene, OR 97402
    541 554 8551

Albany Area
Going Green Compassion Center
    2999 Santiam Hwy Lebanon, OR 97355
    541 405 8856
Four Seasons
30943 Ehlen Drive Albany, OR 97321
    541 704 5326

Oregon Coast Area
Pacific Wave Resource Center
1543 NW 19th St Lincoln City, OR 97367
    541 614 1364

Bend
DiamondTree   2669 NE Twin Knolls Rd Suite 208 Bend, OR
97701   541 706 9340
    Medication Station 817 NW Hill St Bend, OR 97701
        541 550 7777
    Garden Kings OMMP Club   325 NE Franklin Ave Business 97
Bend, OR 97701   541 610 3667

Michigan

MICHIGAN MEDICAL MARIJUANA DISPENSARIES

DETROIT Area

A Detroit Alternative   7340 Grand River Ave Detroit, MI 48204
    313 285 9341

Ant Farm Compassion Club   Delivery
    888 369 3320

Chronic Releaf Wellness Center
    21651 W 8 Mile Rd Detroit, MI 48219
    313 693 4564

Eastside Alternative   17401 Mack Ave Detroit, MI 48224
    855 469 6337

Green Field Collective   15601 Grand River Ave Detroit, MI 48227
    313 272 0395

Green Greener Grow   14631 W 8 Mile Rd Detroit, MI 48235
    248 266 0790

Green Leaf Care Center 5820 N Canton Center Road Canton, MI
48187   734 667 3102

Green Relief 586   Delivery   855 PRO GROW

Green Solutions   1258 South Commerce Walled Lake, MI 48390
    248 859 5297

Green Soul Wellness   22635 Plymouth Rd Detroit, MI 48239
313 444 3044

Green Vibrance Collective   Delivery
734 635 2589

Happy Meds Delivery   734 309 2253

Hardcore Harvest South 24623 Grand River Ave Detroit, MI 48219
313 766 6477

Helping Hand Holistic Center 20245 Van Dyke Ave Detroit, MI
48234   313 733 6693

Medicated Menu Delivery Service
Delivery   248 701 4408

Michigan Alternative Medicine
18422 Woodward Ave Detroit, MI 48203
888 910 6337

Michigan Chronic Relief 18207 West 8 Mile Rd Detroit, MI 48219
313 693 9061

Michigan Wellness Group   16900 W Warren Detroit, MI 48228
313 436 1912

Mile High Awareness And Wellness
24520 West Mcnichols Detroit, MI 48219
313 766 5409

Nature's Alternative   15837 Mack Ave Detroit, MI 48224
313 885 0000

Original Green Health Center 13600 E 8 Mile Rd Suite A Detroit,
MI 48205 313 469 6325

Plan B Wellness Center 20103 W 8 Mile Rd Detroit, MI 48219
248 470 4638

Radicle 7615 W Vernor Detroit, MI 48209
313 406 2245

Relief Choices   21586 Dequindre Rd Warren, MI 48091
800 375 7850

Shake And Bake   20477 Schaefer Hwy Detroit, MI 48235
313 340 2253
Stoney Creek Station   50625 Mound Road Shelby Township, MI
48317   586 321 1518
Taste Buds   8500 E 8 Mile Rd Detroit, MI 48234
248 382 8379
TeleGreen   23695 W 7 Mile Rd Detroit, MI 48219
313 828 6985
The Medicine Cabinet LLC   19307 W Warren Detroit, MI 48228
248 602 6005
TransLove Energies   1486 Gratiot Ave Detroit, MI 48207
313 262 1886
Tree Delivery Service   Delivery
248 325 8194
Urban Genetics   17931 E Warren Detroit, MI 48224
313 821 4259

Ann Arbor Area
3rd Coast Compassion Center
19 North Hamilton Ypsilanti, MI 48197
734 487 5402
Ann Arbor Health Patient Collective
3060 Packard Suite F Ann Arbor, MI 48108
734 929 5645
Ann Arbor Wellness Collective
321 E Liberty St Ann Arbor, MI 48104
734 929 2602
Arborside Compassion 1818 Packard Street Ann Arbor, MI 48104
734 213 1420
CannaCure   50 Ecorse Rd Suite B Ypsilanti, MI 48198
734 484 1990

Cannoisseur Collective Delivery
  734 494 0772
Depot Town Dispensary35 East Cross St Ypsilanti, MI 48198
  734 340 2941
Green Planet Patient Collective
  700 Tappan Ann Arbor, MI 48104
  734 845 2172
Green Vibrance Collective   Delivery
  734 635 2589
Happy Meds Delivery   734 309 2253
Herbal Solutions   124 West Michigan Ave Ypsilanti, MI 48197
  734 487 8421
Medical Garden Solutions   Delivery
  734-945-5063
OM of Medicine   112 S Main St Third Floor Ann Arbor, MI 48104
  734 369 8255
Plymouth Holistic Health Collective
  Delivery   734 459 4950
Sticky   1090 N Huron River Dr Ypsilanti, MI 48197
  734 879 1204
Treecity Health Collective   2730 Jackson Ave Ann Arbor, MI
48103   734 369 3212

Flint Area
Hemphill Wellness Center   3365 Associates Dr Burton, MI
48529   810 820 3812
Michigan Compassion Center
  1222 Glenwood Ave Flint, MI 48503
  970 509 0781
Michigan Organic Solutions   3549 S Dort Hwy Suite 106 Flint, MI
48507   810 309 0564

We Grow   2849 Miller Rd Flint, MI 48457
   810 350 2064
We Grow   305 ½ E State St Montrose, MI 48457
   810 350 2064

Lansing Area
Associates Of Michigans Green Market
   4708 Okemos Rd Okemos, MI 48864
   517 391 0526
Canna Plus Care   2000 W Ganson Jackson, MI 49202
   517 962 5228
Green Leaf Clinic 900 W Holmes Rd Lansing, MI 48910
   517 977 0725
Quality Alternative Medicine 1202 S Washington Ave Lansing, MI
48910   517 574 4316
The Herbal Connection 4314 S Cedar Lansing, MI 48910
   517 977 0511
Tombo's Dispensary N Stuff 4114 Occidental Hwy Adrian, MI
49221   517 528 9139
The MMM Alliance 7555 Us Hwy 12 Onsted, MI 49265
   517 467 5443

Grand Rapids Area
Battle Creek Compassionate Care Center
   1039 Territorial Rd West Battle Creek, MI 49015
   269 964 8770
Eco Options Services   741 Kenmoor Ave Suite D Grand Rapids,
MI 49546 616 285 8080
Great Turtle Delivery   Delivery
   616 566 6656
Great Turtle Emporium 3383 Blue Star Hwy Saugatuck, MI 49453

616 566 6656

Lakeshore Alternatives 6155 Blue Star Hwy Saugatuck, MI 49453
   269 857 1188

Pure West   840 N Black River Dr Ste 80 Holland, MI 49424
   616 466 4204

The Mix   350 28th St SE Grand Rapids, MI 49548
   616 403 1970

Western Michigan Alternative Medical
   113 Union Street S Battle Creek, MI 49017
   269 339 3622

Northern Michigan

Blue Spruce Gallery   8838 Boon Rd Cadillac, MI 49601
   231 258 6607

Cedars Compassion Club   250 ½ South Cedar Street Kalkaska,
MI 49646 231 258 6607

Interlochen Alternative Health
   2074 M137 Interlochen, MI 49643
   231 276 3311

Natural Remedies 1349 S Otsego Ave Suite 1 Gaylord, MI 49735
   989 748 4420

Northern Michigan Caregivers
   5511 North Red Oak Rd Lewiston, MI 49756
   989 786 9636

Northern Specialty Health Houghton
   902 Razorback Dr Suite 10 Houghton, MI 49931
   906 523 5122

Safe Access Compassion Services
   Delivery   715 923 6927

Select Provisions   207 W Grandview Parkway Suite 106 Traverse
City, MI 49684 231 218 7534

Summer Island   1632 N Mitchell St Cadillac, MI 49601
   231 468 3168
Superior Green Collective   1699 S Otsego Suite 1 Gaylord, MI
49735   989 705 2322
Vanderbilt Holistic Apothecary
   7800 Mill St Vanderbilt, MI 49795
   989 983 2530

Colorado

COLORADO: MEDICAL AND RECREATIONAL DISPENSARIES

3D Cannabis Center 4305 Brighton Blvd Denver, CO 80216
303-297-1657

Acme Healing Center – Ridgway
157 US Hwy 550 Ridgway, CO 81432
970-626-4099

Acme Healing Center – Crested Butte
309 Belleview Ave. Crested Butte, CO
970-349-5550

Advanced Medical Alternatives
1269 Elati Street Denver, CO, 80204
303-993-4547

Alpenglow Botanicals   1805 Airport Road Breckenridge CO
80424   970-389-6839

Alpine Wellness   300 W. Colorado Ave. Suite 2C Telluride, CO
81435   (970) 728-1834

AlterMeds   1156 W Dillon Rd #3 Louisville, CO 80027
720-389-6313

Alternative Medical Supplies 9 Karlann Dr. Black Hawk, CO 80422
303-582-0420

Alternative Medicine On Capitol Hill

1301 Marion St Denver, CO 80218

720-961-0560

Altitude Dispensary East   6858 E Evans Ave Denver, CO, 80224   303-756-8888

Altitude Dispensary West   1568 S Federal Blvd. Denver, CO, 80219   720-708-5428

Annie's 135 Nevada St. Central City, CO 80427

(303) 582-5171

Best Colorado Meds   4800 Lamar Street Wheat Ridge, CO 80033   (720) 205-5314

BotanaCare 21+   11450 Cherokee St. Unit A-6 Northglenn, CO, 80234   (303) 254-4200

Botanico   3054 Larimer St Denver, CO 80205

(303) 297-2273

Breckenridge Cannabis Club 226 S Main Street Breckenridge, CO 80424   970-453-4900

Cannabis Care Wellness Center

2515 7th Ave Garden City, CO 80631

CannaMart Denver   3700 W. Quincy Ave., Denver, CO 80236

303-734-0420

Cannasseur 41 N Precision Drive Pueblo West, Colorado

719-647-8924

Caregivers For Life   310 Saint Paul St Denver, Co. 80206

720-536-5462

Choice Organics   813 Smithfield Drive, Unit B Fort Collins, CO 80524   (970) 472-6337

Citi-Med   1640 East Evans Ave. Denver, CO 80210

303-975-6485

Colorado Alternative Medicine

2394 S Broadway Denver CO 80210

(720) 379 - 7295

Colorado Care Facility   5130 East Colfax Avenue Denver, CO 80220-1302   (303) 953-8503

Colorado Harvest Company   1178 S. Kalamath St. Denver, CO 80223   303-777-1840

Compassionate Pain Management
    1116-7 W. Dillon Rd. Louisville, CO 80027
    (303) 665-5596

Dank Colorado   3835 Elm Street DENVER, CO 80207
    (303) 394-3265

Delilah 115 W. Colorado Ave, Telluride, CO 81435
    970 728 5880

Denco 3460 Park Ave West Denver, CO 80216
    303-433-2266

Denver Kush Club 2615 Welton St Denver, CO 80202
    303-736-6550

Doctors Garden Dispensary   580 Main St # 300 Carbondale, CO 81623   (970) 963-9323

Euflora 401 16th Street Mall Denver, Colorado 80202
    (303) 534-6255

Evergreen Apothecary   1568 South Broadway Denver, CO 80210
    (303) 722-1227

Fox Street Wellness   4773 Fox Street, Denver, CO
    720-881-7460

Fresh Baked 2539 Pearl St. Boulder, CO 80302
    (303)440-9393

Frosted Leaf - Federal   445 Federal Blvd. Denver CO
    303.355.4372

GAIA East Denver 5926 E Colfax Ave Denver, CO 80220
    303-573-6337

Good Chemistry   330 E COLFAX AVE DENVER, CO 80203
    720.524.4657

Green Dragon – Aspen 400 E. Hyman Ave., Unit 1A Aspen, CO
81611   970.429.4035
Green Dragon – Glenwood Springs
   1420 Devereux Rd. Glenwood Springs, CO 81601
   970.230.9057
Green Grass 440 Lawrence St Central City, CO 80427
   303-582-5088
Greenwerkz – Edgewater   5840 W. 25th Ave Edgewater, CO
80214   (303) 647-5209
Greenwerkz – Glenwood Springs
   2922 S. Glen Ave. Glenwood Springs, CO 81601
   970-366-4600
Hashish House   428 S. McCulloch Blvd. Pueblo West CO. 81007
   719-547-1009
Healing House Denver 2383 S. Downing St. Denver, CO 80210
   720-379-3816
Herbal Bliss 842 North Summit Blvd. #13 Frisco, CO
   (970) 668-3514
Herbal Wellness   400 West S Boulder Rd. #2700 Lafayette Co.
80026   303-665-5599
Herbs Nest   3900 E 48th Ave Denver, CO 80216
   303-246-0380
High Country Healing   191 Blue River PKWY #202 Silverthorne,
Colorado 80498   (970) 468-7858
High Country Healing – Alma
   40 S. Main St. Alma, CO 80420
   719-836-9000
High Level Health On Lincoln
   970 Lincoln Street, Denver, CO
   (303) 839-9333
iVita Wellness – Franklin   3980 Franklin St. Denver, Colorado

303-952-9150

iVita Wellness - Pearl   1660 Pearl St Denver, CO 80203
303-952-9150

Karing Kind   5854 Rawhide Ct. Unit C Boulder, Co 80302
303-449-WEED

L'Eagle 380 Quivas Street Denver, Colorado 80223
303-825-0497

Lightshade - Peoria   11975 E. 40TH AVE. DENVER, CO 80239
303-468-6100

Lightshade Holly   3950 HOLLY ST. DENVER CO. 80207
303-468-6100

Lodo Wellness Center   1617 Wazee Street, Unit B Denver, CO
80202   303-534-5020

Marisol Therapeutics   922 E Kimble Dr Pueblo West, CO 81007
719-547-4000

Medical MJ Supply   4845 Van Gordon St. Wheat Ridge, CO
80033   303-997-4082

Medicinal Oasis   6359 E Evans Ave Denver, CO 80222
303.756.1494

Medicinal Wellness Center   5430 W 44th Avenue Mountain View,
CO, 80212   303-333-3338

Medicine Man   4750 Nome St, Unit B, Denver, CO 80239
(303) 373-0752

Metro Cannabis   8151 E Colfax Ave Denver, CO 80220?
(720) 771-9866

Milagro Wellness   1181 County Road 308 Dumont, CO 80436
(720) 379-3672

Mile High Recreational Cannabis
1705 Federal Blvd Denver CO, 80204
303-455-9333

MMJ America - LoDo   2042 Arapahoe Street Denver, CO 80205

(720) 242-9308

Mountain Medicinals Wellness Center
1800 Colorado Blvd., #5 Idaho Springs, CO 80452
303-567-4211

Native Roots Apothecary   910 16th Street, Suite 805 Denver, Colorado 80202

Natural Remedies 1620 Market St., Suite 5W Denver, CO 80202
303-953-0884

Nature's Spirit   113 E. 7th Street Leadville, CO 80461
(719) 486-1900

Natures Herbs and Wellness Center
522 27th Street Garden City, CO 80631
(970) 353-1170

Northern Lights   2045 Sheridan Blvd Edgewater, CO 80214
303-274-6495

Options Medical Center - Boulder
1534 55?th St. Boulder, CO. 80303
303.444.0861

Options Medical Center - Wheat Ridge
9085 W 44th Ave Wheat Ridge, CO 80033
720.242.9452

Organix   1795 Airport Rd? Breckenridge, CO 80424
(970) 453-1340

Patient's Choice - Broadway 2251 S. Broadway Denver, CO 80210
303-862-5016

Patients Choice - Edgewater 2517 Sheridan Blvd Edgewater, CO 80214   720.920.9617

Patients Choice - Morrison Road
4000 Morrison Rd Denver, CO 80219
303-997-4602

Pink House Mile High   2008 Federal Blvd. Denver, CO 80211

303-656-9697

Pueblo West Organics   609 East Enterprise Drive, Ste 140
   Pueblo West, CO 81007

Rocky Mountain High – LoDo
   1538 Wazee St. Denver, CO 80202
   (303) 623-7246

Rocky Mountain Remedies   2730 Downhill Plaza #106
Steamboat Springs, CO 80487   970-871-2768

Sacred Seed 5885 E. Evans Ave. Denver, CO 80222
   (303) 756-3762

Serene Wellness – Empire   13 East Park Ave Empire, CO, 80438
   (303) 569-2011

Sergeant Green Leaf Wellness Center
   1402 Argentine St. Georgetown, CO 80444
   (303) 569-0444

Silverpeak Apothecary 520 E. Cooper Ave. Aspen, CO
   970-925-4372

Soma Wellness Lounge 423 Belleview Ave. Crested Butte, CO
81224   (970) 349-6640

Starbuds   4690 Brighton Blvd Denver, CO 80216
   720.387.8952

Stash   300 Aspen Airport Business Center Suite B Aspen,
Colorado, 81611   970-925-6468

Sticky Buds – Alameda 183 W Alameda Ave Denver, CO 80220
   (303) 736-6999

Sticky Buds – Broadway   2262 S Broadway Denver, CO 80210
   (303) 282-0200

Sunrise Solutions 43 Main St. Bailey, CO 80421
   303.816.MEDS

Sweet Leaf   5100 W 38th Ave Denver, CO 80212
   (303) 480-5323

Sweet Leaf Pioneer   1286 Chambers Ave Suite 105 Eagle, CO 81631   (970)328-9060

Telluride Bud Company   135 South Spruce St Telluride, CO 81435   970.239.6039

Telluride Green Room   250 South Fir St Telluride, CO 81435 (970) 728-7999

Terrapin Care Station   1795 Folsom St. Boulder, CO 80302 303.954.8402 x1

The Clinic Colorado   3888 E. Mexico Ave Denver, CO 80210 303.758.9114

The Farm   2801 Iris Avenue Boulder, CO 80301 (303)440-1323

The Giving Tree of Denver   2707 W. 38th Ave. Denver, CO 80211   303-477-8888

The Grass Station 4125 Elati Street Denver, CO 80216

The Green Depot 2020 S. Broadway Denver, CO 80210 303-728-9962

The Green Room 2750 Glenwood Dr Boulder, CO 80304 (303) 945-4074

The Green Solution - Denver
2601 W. Alameda Avenue Denver, CO 80219
303.990.9723

The Green Solution - Denver East
4400 Grape Street Denver, CO 80216
303.990.9723

The Green Solution - Northglenn
470 Malley Drive Northglenn, CO 80233
303.990.9723

The Greener Side 3321 S. Interstate 25 Pueblo, CO 81004 (719) 251-4638

The Greenest Green   5290 Arapahoe Ave Boulder, CO 80303

(303) 953-2852

The Grove   74 Federal Blvd. Denver, CO 80219
(720) 502-3957

The Haven   777 Canosa Ct. #102 Denver, CO 80204
(303)534-2600

The Health Center Uptown   1736 Downing St Denver, CO 80218
(303) 758-9997

The Highway   1221 Country Road 308 Downieville, CO 80436
720.242.8692

The Kind Room   1881 S Broadway, Denver, CO 80210
720-266-3136

The Kine Mine   2820 Colorado Blvd Idaho Springs, CO 80452
303-567-2018

The Sanctuary   5110 Race St. Denver, CO 80216
(720) 420-7604

The Shelter   4095 Jackson St. Denver, CO 80216
720) 266-5215

The Spot   748 E Industrial Blvd Pueblo West, CO 81007
(719) 547-8011

The Spring   15 Colorado Blvd. Idaho Springs, CO 80452
(303) 567-2706

Timberline Herbal Clinic & Wellness Center
3995 E 50th Ave Denver, CO 80223
303-322-0901

Urba   2609 Walnut St Denver, CO 80205
(720) 328-2227

Village Green Society   2043 16TH ST, BOULDER, CO 80302
720-389-5726

Walking Raven   2001 S Broadway Denver, CO 80210
(720) 327-5613

Wellness Center of Denver   330 S. Dayton St. Denver, Colorado

80247   (303) 665-4968?
  Wellspring   1724 S. Broadway Denver, CO 80210
    303-733-3113
  Xg Platinum 2506 6th Ave Garden City, CO 80631
    (970) 352-4119

Denver Metro Medical Marijuana Dispensaries
303   155 N Federal Blvd Denver, CO 80219
  720 542 9434
3D Denver's Discreet Dispensary LLC
  4305 Brighton Blvd Denver, CO 80216
  303 297 1657
420 Wellness 543 Bryant St Denver, CO 80204
  303 996 9922
420 Wellness 2426 South Federal Blvd Denver, CO 80236
  303 493 1787
A Cut Above 1911 S Broadway Denver, CO 80210
  720 536 8965
A Cut Off The Top 2059 W 9th Ave Denver, CO 80204
  303 825 9227
Advanced Medical Alternatives
  1269 Elati St Denver, CO 80204
  303 993 4547
Alameda Wellness 183 W Alameda Ave Denver, CO 80223
  303 736 6999
Allgreens   762 Kalamath St Denver, CO 80204
  303 658 0107
Alternative Medicine   1301 Marion St Denver, CO 80218
  720 961 0560
Altitude 6858 E Evans Ave Denver, CO 80224

303 756 8888

Altitude1568 S Federal Blvd Denver, CO 80219
720 708 5428

Altitude Wellness Center   3435 South Yosemite St Suite #200
Denver, CO 80231   303 751 7888

AMA Denver MMC 4283 W Florida Ave Denver, CO 80219
303 922 9139

Artisanal Medicinals   2042 S Bannock St Denver, CO 80223
720 583 1358

At Home Remedies Inc 4735 W 38th Ave Denver, CO 80212
303 455 0079

Back To The Garden   1755 S Broadway Denver, CO 80210
720 583 2119

Ballpark Holistic Dispensary 2119 Larimer St Denver, CO 80205
303 996 6884

Best Colorado Meds   4800 Lamar St Wheat Ridge, CO 80033
720 205 5314

BotanaCare MMC   11450 Cherokee St Unit A7 Northglenn, CO
80234   303 254 4200

Botanico   3054 Larimer St Denver, CO 80205
303 297 2273

Bud Cellar   1450 S Santa Fe Dr Unit 102 Denver, CO 80223
303 777 6644

Bud Med Health Centers   2517 Sheridan Blvd Edgewater, CO
80214   720 920 9617

Buddies Wellness 1270 W Ceder Ave Unit A Denver, CO 80223
720 475 1983

Burnzwell   4751 East 46th Ave Denver, CO 80216
303 322 5555

Cannabis Station 1201 20th St Denver, CO 80202
303 297 WEED

CannaMart   3700 W Quincy Ave Unit 3702 Denver, CO 80236
303 734 0420
CannaMart   1086 W Littleton Blvd Littleton, CO 80120
720 627 5091
Caregivers For Life   310 Saint Paul St Denver, CO 80206
720 536 5462
Chronorado Medical   6625 Leetsdale Dr #A Denver, CO 80224
303 951 5151
CitiMed 1640 East Evans Ave Denver, CO 80210
303 975 6485
Colorado Care Facility   5130 E Colfax Ave Denver, CO 80220
303 953 8503
Colorado Alternative Medicine
2394 S Broadway Denver, CO 80210
720 379 7295
Colorado Dank   3835 Elm St Suite B Denver, CO 80207
303 394 3265
Colorado Harvest Company   1178 South Kalamath Denver, CO
80223   303 777 1840
Colorado Harvest Moon 1890 South Wadsworth Blvd Denver, CO
80232   303 986 8800
Compassionate Pain Managment
1585 Quail St Unit 13B Lakewood, CO 80215
303 232 3620
Cure   6200 East Yale Ave Denver, CO 80222
720 296 2857
DENCO Alternative Medicine 3460 Park Ave West Unit D Denver,
CO 80216 303 433 2266
Denver Dispensary   4975 Vasquez Blvd Denver, CO 80216
303 308 1111
Denver Kush Club 2615 Welton St Denver, CO 80205

303 736 6550

Denver Patients Center 2070 S Huron Street Denver, CO 80223
303 733 3977

Denver Patients Group 2863 Larimer St Unit B Denver, CO 80205
303 484 1662

Denver Relief1 Broadway #A150 Denver, CO 80203
303 420 MEDS

DenverDam 4571 Ivy St Denver, CO 80216
303 951 1480

Doctors Orders   1406 West 38th Ave Denver, CO 80221
303 433 0276

Element420 82 S Federal Blvd Denver, CO 80219
303 945 4774

Emerald City Organics 5115 N Federal Blvd Suite 9 Denver, CO
80221   303 458 1210

Emerald City Organics 120 S Kalamath St Denver, CO 80223
303 777 5252

Evergreen Apothecary 1568 South Broadway Denver, CO 80210
303 722 1227

Expanding Universe   3814 Walnut St Denver, CO 80205
303 308 0420

Flavored Essentials   3955 Oneida St Denver, CO 80207
303 377 0539

Fox Street Wellness   4773 Fox Street Denver, CO 80216
720 881 7460

Frosted Leaf 6302 East Colfax Ave Denver, CO 80220
720 328 0758

Frosted Leaf 445 Federal Blvd Denver, CO 80204
303 355 4372

Frosted Leaf 50 Lipan St Denver, CO 80223
303 993 5466

Frosted Leaf 11 W Hampden Ave Englewood, CO 80110
303 862 4305
Gala Plant Based Medicine   5926 East Colfax Ave Denver, CO
80220   303 573 6337
Ganja Gourmet   1810 S Broadway Denver, CO 80210
303 282 9333
Garden Of The Gods   5050 York Street Denver, CO 80216
303 292 3383
Garden Of The Gods   468 S Federal Blvd Denver, CO 80219
303 936 0309
Gobeville Meds   4837 Washington St Denver, CO 80216
303 953 2156
Good Chemistry   330 East Colfax Denver, CO 80202
720 524 4657
Good Meds Englewood 3431 S Federal Blvd Englewood, CO
80110   303 761 9170
Good Meds Lakewood   8420 W Colfax Ave Lakewood, CO 80214
303 238 1253
Grassroots Grown 4379 Tejon St Denver, CO 80211
303 420 6279
Green Around You970 S Oneida Suite 17 Denver, CO 80224
303 284 9075
Green Cross Caregivers 1842 S Parker Rd Unit 18 Denver, CO
80231   303 337 2229
Green Depot 2020 S Broadway Denver, CO 80210
303 728 9962
Green Man Cannabis   1355 Santa Fe Drive Suite F Denver, CO
80204   720 842 4842
Green Man Cannabis   4380 S Syracuse St Suite 310 Denver, CO
80237   720 382 5950
Green Mountain Care   5423 S Prince St Littleton, CO 80120

303 862 6571

Green Solution   4400 Grape St Denver, CO 80216
303 990 9723

Greenfields   1798 W Mississippi Ave Denver, CO 80223
303 455 1795

Greenwerkz Custer Place   1131 West Custer Place Unit #A
Denver, CO 80223   303 647 5156

Greenwerkz Edgewater 5840 W 25th Ave Edgewater, CO 80214
303 647 5210

GroundSwell 3121 East Colfax Denver, CO 80206
303 309 0078

Healing House   2383 S Downing Street Denver, CO 80210
720 379 3816

Healing House   10712 W Alameda Ave Lakewood, CO 80226
303 988 5255

Health Depot4615 E Colfax Ave Denver, CO 80220
720 398 8805

Herbal Alternatives   2568 South Broadway Denver, CO 80210
303 955 1143

Herbal Connections   2209 W 32nd Ave Denver, CO 80211
720 999 6295

Herbal Remedies Denver   5109 W Alameda Ave Denver, CO
80219   303 742 0420

Herban Medicinals70 Broadway St Suite 50 Denver, CO 80203
720 343 HERB

Herbs Nest MMJ Dispensary 3900 E 48th Ave Denver, CO 80216
303 246 7360

Herbs4You   20 E 9th Ave Denver, CO 80203
303 830 9999

High Level Health 2028 E Colfax Denver, CO 80206
303 355 WEED

High Level Health 970 Lincoln Denver, CO 80203
303 839 WEED
High Street Growers   330 N Federal Blvd Denver, CO 80219
720 583 0194
Higher Ground   2215 E Mississippi Ave Denver, CO 80210
303 733 5500
Holistic Life   1395 S Sheridan Blvd Lakewood, CO 80232
303 935 2839
Infinite Wellness Center 1701 Kipling St Lakewood, CO 80214
720 458 0277
iVita Wellness   1660 Pearl St Denver, CO 80203
303 952 9150
Jane Medicals   7380 E Colfax Ave Denver, CO 80220
303 388 5263
Jane Medicals   9202 W Alameda Ave Lakewood, CO 80226
303 763 5263
Karmaceuticals   4 S Santa Fe Drive Denver, CO 80223
303 765 2762
Kind Love   4380 East Alameda Ave Denver, CO 80246
303 565 3600
Kind Pain Management 2636 Youngfield St Lakewood, CO 80215
303 237 5463
Kindman   4125 Elati St Denver, CO 80216
303 546 3626
Kushism   2527 Federal Blvd Denver, CO 80211
303 477 0772
L'Eagle Services   380 Quivas St Denver, CO 80223
303 825 0497
LaContes   5194 Washington St Denver, CO 80216
303 292 2252
LeContes   105 E 7th Ave Denver, CO 80203

303 292 2252

Lightshade Labs   3950 North Holly St Denver, CO 80207
303 468 6100

Lightshade Labs   11975 40th Ave Denver, CO 80239
720 974 7220

Lincoln Herbal   424 Lincoln St Denver, CO 80203
303 955 0701

Little Green Pharmacy   1331 South Broadway Denver, CO 80210
303 722 2133

Livwell Broadway   432 S Broadway Denver, CO 80209
720 428 2550

Local Product Of Colorado   419 W 13th Ave Denver, CO 80204
303 736 6850

Lodo Wellness Center   1617 Wazee St Unit B Denver, CO 80202
303 534 5020

Lotus Medical   1444 Wazee St Suite 115 Denver, CO 80202
720 974 3109

Lucky 7's   777 Umatilla St Denver, CO 80204
303 893 9333

Lush   2490 West 2nd Ave Unit A Denver, CO 80223
303 880 1554

Medical MJ Supply 4845 Van Gordon St Wheat Ridge, CO 80033
303 997 4082

Medicinal Oasis   6359 E Evans Ave Denver, CO 80222
303 756 1494

Medicinal Wellness Center   5430 W 44th Ave Mountain Valley,
CO 80212 303 333 3338

Medicine Man   4750 Nome St Unit B Denver, CO 80239
303 373 0752

Medicine Man Medical Market Glendale
4966 Leetsdale Glendale, CO 80246

720 389 7442

Metro Cannabis Inc   8151 E Colfax Denver, CO 80220
720 771 9866

Metropolis Medical   4600 Ironton St Denver, CO 80239
303 373 9333

Mile High Dispensary 2 1350 S Sheridan Denver, CO 80232
303 934 6337

Mile High Green Cross 852 N Broadway Denver, CO 80203
303 861 4252

Mile High Medical Cannabis   1705 Federal Blvd Denver, CO
80204   303 455 WEED

Mile High Wellness   3525 S Tamarac Dr Suite 110 Denver, CO
80237   720 382 8516

Mind Body Spirit Wellness Center
6745B West Mississippi Ave Lakewood, CO 80226
303 934 9750

MMD of Colorado 2609 Walnut St Denver, CO 80205
303 736 9642

MMJ America Downtown   2042 Arapahoe Street Denver, CO
80205   720 242 9308

MMJ America Golden Triangle
1321 Elati St Denver, CO 80204
303 999 0664

Native Roots Apothecary   910 16th Street Suite 805 Denver,
CO 80202 303 623 1900

Natural Remedies 1620 Market St Suite 5W Denver, CO 80202
303 953 0884

Nature's Kiss 4332 S Broadway Ave Englewood, CO 80113
303 484 9327

Natures Best Alternative Medicine
4601 E Mississippi Ave Glendale, CO 80246

303 386 3185

New Age Medical   2553 Sheridan Blvd Edgewater, CO 80214
303 233 1322

Next Harvest 2748 W Alameda Denver, CO 80219
303 936 5983

Northern Lights Natural RX   2045 Sheridan Blvd Edgewater, CO
80214   303 274 6495

Northwest Wellness Center   4707 Lipan St Denver, CO 80211
303 321 3010

Patients Choice   4000 Morrison Road Denver, CO 80219
303 997 4602

Patients Choice of Colorado 2251 S Broadway Denver, CO 80210
303 862 5016

Patients Choice of Colorado 7063 W Colfax Ave Lakewood, CO
80214   303 233 3901

Peace In Medicine Center   2647 West 38th Ave Denver, CO
80211   303 455 1119

Personalized Organic Treatments
219 Vallejo St Denver, CO 80223
303 777 1550

Physician Preferred Products 2100 E 112th Ave Northglenn, CO
80233   303 974 5966

Pink House Cherry 111 S Madison St #111 Denver, CO 80209
303 399 MEDS

Pink House Mile High   2008 Federal Blvd Denver, CO 80211
303 656 9697

Pink House Pearl   1445 S Pearl St Denver, CO 80210
303 733 6337

Pink House Riverside   3722 Chestnut Place Denver, CO 80216
720 381 0214

Platte Valley Dispensary 2301 7th St Denver, CO 80211

303 953 0295

PostModern Health   5660 W Alameda Ave Lakewood, CO 80226   303 922 9479

Preferred Organic Therapy And Wellness
1569 S Colorado Blvd Denver, CO 80222
303 867 4768

Pure Medical Dispensary   1133 Bannock St Denver, CO 80204
303 534 7873

Remedy Care Center Solace Meds
1850 S Federal Blvd Denver, CO 80219
303 935 2694

Rino Supply Company   3100 Blake St Denver, CO 80205
303 296 2680

Rocky Mountain High   1538 Wazee St Denver, CO 80202
303 623 7246

Rocky Mountain High   1233 W Alameda Ave Denver, CO 80223
720 941 7246

Rocky Mountain Organic Medicine
511 Orchard St Golden, CO 80401
720 230 9111

Southwest Alternative Care   1075 S Fox Street Denver, CO 80223
303 593 2931

Southwest Alternative Care   3937 West Colfax Ave Denver, CO 80204   720 287 3934

Standing Akimbo 3801 Jason St Denver, CO 80211
303 997 4526

Starbuds   4690 Brighton Blvd Denver, CO 80216
720 387 8952

Sticky Buds   2262 South Broadway Denver, CO 80210
303 282 0200

Summit Wellness 2117 Larimer St Denver, CO 80205

720 407 8112

Sweet Leaf Inc   5100 W 38th Ave Denver, CO 80212
303 480 5323

Tetra Hydro Center LLC 9206 East Hampden Ave Denver, CO
80237   303 221 0331

The Clinic   745 E 6th Ave Denver, CO 80203
720 536 5229

The Clinic   4625 E Colfax Denver, CO 80220
303 333 3644

The Clinic   3460 W 32nd Ave Denver, CO 80211
303 997 7130

The Clinic   3888 E Mexico Ave #110 Denver, CO 80210
303 758 9114

The Clinic   3600 S Wadsworth Blvd Lakewood, CO 80235
303 484 8853

The Clone Store   755 South Federal Blvd Unit 5 Denver, CO
80219   303 993 5653

The Giving Tree of Denver   2707 W 38th Ave Denver, CO 80211
303 477 8888

The Golden Goat   7801 E Colfax Ave Denver, CO 80220
720 542 3145

The Green Solution   2601 W Alameda Denver, CO 80219
303 990 9723

The Green Solution   470 Malley Drive Northglenn, CO 80233
303 990 9723

The Green Solution   389 Wadsworth Blvd Lakewood, CO
80226   303 990 9723

The Grove   74 Federal Blvd Denver, CO 80219
720 502 3957

The Haven   777 Canosa Court #102 Denver, CO 80204
303 534 2600

The Health Center U-Hills   2777 S Colorado Blvd Denver, CO
80222   303 758 9997

The Health Center Uptown   1736 Downing St Denver, CO 80218
303 758 9997

The Health Joint   4401 Zenobia St Denver, CO 80212
303 433 9333

The Healthy Choice Wellness Center
3005 W Gill Place Denver, CO 80219
303 922 4842

The Hemp Center 2430 W Main St Littleton, CO 80120
303 993 7824

The Herbal Cure   1909 South Broadway Denver, CO 80210
303 719 4372

The Herbal Cure   985 S Logan St Denver, CO 80209
303 777 9333

The Releaf Center 2000 West 32nd Ave Denver, CO 80211
303 458 5323

The Retreat   2420 S Colorado Blvd Denver, CO 80222
720 974 9327

The Ridge   10185 W 49th Ave Wheat Ridge, CO 80033
720 508 4827

The Sanctuary   5110 Race St Denver, CO 80216
720 420 7604

The Wellness Shop   5885 E Evans Ave Denver, CO 80222
303 756 3762

Timberline Herbal Clinic And Wellness
3995 East 50th Ave Denver, CO 80216
303 322 0901

Trenchtown Medical Marijuana Center
734 Sheridan Blvd Denver, CO 80214
303 495 3531

Universal Herbs   800 Park Ave West Denver, CO 80205
303 756 1414

Urban Dispensary 2675 West 38th Ave Denver, CO 80211
720 389 9179

Verde Wellness Center 5101 E Colfax Ave Denver, CO 80220
303 474 4489

Very Best Medicine   6853 Leetsdale Drive Denver, CO 80224
720 941 8872

VIP Cannabis 2949 W Alameda Ave Denver, CO 80219
720 379 3615

VIP Dispensary   1515 Adams St Denver, CO 80206
720 389 9375

Walking Raven   2001 South Broadway Denver, CO 80210
720 327 5613

Wellness Center of Denver   330 S Dayton Denver, CO 80247
303 856 7798

Wellspring Collective   1724 S Broadway Denver, CO 80210
303 733 3113

Colorado Springs Area

A Cut Above 1150 E Fillmore St Colorado Springs, CO 80907
719 434 1665

A Cut Above 3750 Astrozon Blvd Ste #140 Colorado Springs, CO
80910   719 391 5099

A Wellness Center 2918 Wood Ave Colorado Springs, CO 80907
719 375 1907

Absolute Manitou Wellness   2 Manitou Ave Manitou Springs, CO
80829   719 645 8881

Advance Cure for Vera Bestura LLC
2755 Ore Mill Rd Ste 13 Colorado Springs, CO 80904
719 505 8288

Alternative Medicine Colorado Springs
2606 W Colorado Ave Colorado Springs, CO 80904
719 358 6955
Altitude Organic Medicine   523 South Tejon St Colorado
Springs, CO 80903   719 313 9841
Amendment 20 Caregivers   2727 Palmer Park Blvd Colorado
Springs, CO 80909   719 375 5610
American Wellness Center   3632 W Colorado Ave Colorado
Springs, CO 80904   719 630 5075
Best Budz   3729 Austin Bluffs Parkway Colorado Springs, CO
80918   719 598 0168
Bijou Wellness Center   2132 E Bijou St Ste 114 Colorado Springs,
CO 80909 719 465 2407
Briargate Wellness Center LLC
890 Dublin Blvd Suite C Colorado Springs, CO 80918
719 598 3510
Broadmoor Wellness Center   1414 S Tejon St Colorado Springs,
CO 80905 719 634 0420
Canna Meds Wellness Center 2363 N Academy Blvd Colorado
Springs, CO 80909   719 638 6337
Cannabicare 1466 Woolsey Heights Colorado Springs, CO 80915
719 573 2262
Cannabis Therapeutics 907 E Fillmore St Colorado Springs, CO
80907   719 633 7124
Discreet Treats   101 N Tejon Ste 102 Colorado Springs, CO
80903   719 633 5947
Discreet Treats   288 South Academby Blvd Ste C Colorado
Springs, CO 80910   719 630 2137
Doctors Orders   2106 E Boulder St Colorado Springs, CO 80909
719 634 8808
Eagles Nest Wellness Center 8455 W Hwy 24 Cascade, CO 80809

719 687 2928

East West Alternative Medicine

1905 N Academy Suite B Colorado Springs, CO 80909

719 574 3997

Enlightened Care   1330 Garden of the Gods Rd Colorado Springs, CO 80907 719 531 7079

EZ Natural Alternatives 3475 Pine Tree Square Ste E Colorado Springs, CO 80909   719 694 9384

Front Range Alternative 5913 North Nevada Ave Colorado Springs, CO 80918 719 213 0118

Gaia Plant Based Medicine   417 North Circle Drive Colorado Springs, CO 80909   719 597 4429

Green And Healthy Wellness LLC

212 S 21st St Colorado Springs, CO 80904

719 465 1331

Green Pharm LLC 325 Delaware Dr Colorado Springs, CO 80909

719 591 2070

Grow Life   1516 Dustry Dr Colorado Springs, CO 80905

719 635 1700

Humboldt Care And Wellness Center

6823 Space Village Ave Colorado Springs, CO 80915

719 591 1004

Humboldt Care And Wellness Center 2

1324 W Garden of the Gods Rd Colorado Springs, CO 80907

719 694 1402

Indispensary 2   3044 W Colorado Ave Colorado Springs, CO 80904   719 203 4592

Indispensary 3   3031 East Platte Ave Colorado Springs, CO 80909   719 203 4542

JP Wellness   1741 South Academy Colorado Springs, CO 80916

719 622 1000

Kind Therapeutics 4058 Palmer Park Colorado Springs, CO 80909
719 637 4096

Levity Wellness   426 West Fillmore Colorado Springs, CO 80907
719 266 5463

Maggie's Farm   1424 S Nevada Ave Colorado Springs, CO
80905   719 328 0420

Maggie's Farm 3   818 E Fillmore Colorado Springs, CO 80907
719 358 8849

Marimeds   222 E Moreno Ave Colorado Springs, CO 80903
719 634 8285

MC Caregivers   6020 Erin Park Dr Suite A Colorado Springs, CO
80918   719 264 6337

Medibis LLC 3701 N Nevada Ave Colorado Springs, CO 80907
719 633 8882

Mile High Holistics   198 County Line Road Palmer Lake, CO
80133   719 487 0901

Mountain Med Club   22 S Chesnut St Colorado Springs, CO
80905   719 533 4180

Natural Mystic Cannabis Caregivers
416 East Colorado Ave Ste 101 Colorado Springs, CO 80903
719 203 5094

NaturaLeaf   1004 S Tejon Colorado Springs, CO 80903
719 630 7300

Nature's Way 5012 N Academy Blvd Colorado Springs, CO 80918
719 531 MEDS

New Horizons   1460 Woolsey Heights Colorado Springs, CO
80915   719 597 7002

Pain Management Solutions   1022 S Royer St Colorado Springs,
CO 80903 719 473 0279

Palmer Lake Wellness Center 850 Commercial Lane Palmer Lake,
CO 80133 719 488 9900

Pikes Peak Alternative Health 1605 South Tejon St Suite 101 Colorado Springs, CO 80905   719 575 9835

Pikes Peak Cannabis Caregivers
    3715 Drennan Road Colorado Springs, CO 80910
    719 216 5452

Pink House Colorado Springs 700 Juanita St Colorado Springs, CO 80909   719 635 4367

Pure Intentions Wellness   201 N Academy Blvd Colorado Springs, CO 80909   719 570 7432

Pure Medical 19 N Tejon St Suite #108 Colorado Springs, CO 80903   719 634 7390

Pure Medical 2   207 Rockrimmon Blvd Unit C Colorado Springs, CO 80919 719 264 0800

Quality Choice Alternative Care Center
    2398 E Boulder Street Colorado Springs, CO 80909
    719 632 5667

Rocky Mountain Medical   616 Arrawanna Colorado Springs, CO 80909 719 337 6132

Rocky Mountain Miracles   2316 E Bijou St Colorado Springs, CO 80909 719 473 9333

Rocky Road Remedies   586 South Academy Blvd Colorado Springs, CO 80910   719 574 4230

Southern Colorado Medical Marijuana
    3410 N Prospect St Colorado Springs, CO 80907
    719 344 5021

Strawberry Fields Alternative Health
    3404 West Colorado Avenue Colorado Springs, CO 80904
    719 471 2837

The 64 Store 502 West Colorado Ave Colorado Springs, CO 80905
    719 602 0640

The Green House   410 S 8th St Unit B Colorado Springs, CO

80905   719 344 5996
The Healing Canna   3692 E Bijou St Colorado Springs, CO 80909   719 637 7645
The Hemp Center 2501 W Colorado Ave #106 Colorado Springs, CO 80904 719 633 1611
The Herb Shoppe 3020 W Colorado Ave Colorado Springs, CO 80904   719 634 MEDS
The Organic Seed 2304 E Platte Ave Colorado Springs, CO 80909   719 465 1846
The Secret Stash   2845 Ore Mill Rd Unit 6 Colorado Springs, CO 80904   719 633 8499
Third Day Apothecary   4865 N Academy Blvd Colorado Springs, CO 80918 719 266 6699
Todays Health Care   975 W Fillmore Colorado Springs, CO 80907   719 633 1300
Todays Health Care II   225 S 8th St Colorado Springs, CO 80905   719 635 9002
Tree Of Wellness MMC 1000 W Fillmore/I-25 Ste 105 Colorado Springs, CO 80907   719 635 5556
Trichome Health Consultants 2117 W Colorado Ave Colorado Springs, CO 80904   719 635 6337
White Mountain Medicine   3234 N Nevada Ave Colorado Springs, CO 80907   719 622 6652
WTJ MMJ Supply   1347 N Academy Colorado Springs, CO 80909   719 646 8208

Pueblo Area
4 Real Cannabis   16878 Hwy 160 Ft Garland CO, 81133   719 989 8221
Alternative Medical Remedies   1450 L St Penrose, CO 81240

719 372 6011

Fremont County Cannabis   1505 Elm Canon City, CO 81212
719 275 1000

Heritage Organics 401 Broadway Ste A Penrose, CO 81240
719 372 6447

High Valley Healing Center   116 S Alder Crestone, CO 81131
719 256 4006

Maggie's Farm 2   3055 US Hwy 50 Ste F Canon City, CO 81212
719 372 1014

Natures Remedy Wellness   749 E Enterprise Dr Pueblo, CO
81007   719 547 8011

Pueblo West Organics   609 E Enterprise Dr Ste 140 Pueblo West,
CO 81007 719 647 2043

Rocky Mountain Cannabis   465 Valley Road Canon City, CO
81212   719 275 6070

Steel City Meds   74 N McCulloch Ave Ste 120 Pueblo West, CO
81007   719 547 5152

The Greener Side 3321 S Interstate 25 Pueblo, CO 81004
719 251 4638

Fort Collins Area
A Kind Place 938 N College Ave Fort Collins, CO 80524
970 282 3811

Cannabis Care Wellness Center
5740 Suite C South College Fort Collins, CO 80525
970 797 2155

Cannabis Care Wellness Center
2515 7th Ave Garden City CO 80631
970 515 5839

Choice Organics   813 Smithfield Dr Unit B Fort Collins, CO
80524   970 472 6337

Cloud Nine Caregivers 2506 6th Ave Garden City, CO 80634
   970 352 4119
Green Tree Berthoud   1090 North 2nd St Berthoud, CO 80504
   970 670 9120
Herbs Medicinals Inc   1015 2nd St Berthoud, CO 80513
   970 344 5060
Infinite Wellness Center 900 North College Ave Fort Collins, CO
80524   970 484 8380
King Care Of Colorado 6617 South College Ave Fort Collins, CO
80525   970 568 8020
LivWell 2647 8th Ave Unit B Garden City, CO 80631
   970 616 6007
Medical MJ Supply 810 N College Ave Fort Collins, CO 80524
   970 484 1695
Natures Herbs And Wellness Center
   522 27th St Garden City, CO 80631
   970 353 1170
Organic Alternatives   346 E Mountain Ave Fort Collins, CO
80524   970 482 7100
Sedgwick Alternative Relief   107 Main Ave Sedgwick, CO 80749
   970 463 5328
Solace Meds 301 Smokey St Unit A Fort Collins, CO 80525
   970 225 6337

Aspen Area
Acme Dispensary 309 Bellview Ave Crested Butte, CO 81224
   970 349 5550
Aspen Roaring Fork Wellness 24505 Hwy 82 Basalt, CO 81621
   970 920 2222
Aspen Silverpeak Apothecary 520 East Cooper Ave LL2 Aspen, CO
81611   970 925 4372

Boom Town Crested Butte Alternative
   310 Belleview Unit #2 Crested Butte, CO 81224
   970 456 5384
Colorado Alternative Health Care
   125 Peach Ave Palisade, CO 81526
   970 424 5844
Crested Butte Wellness Center
   329 Belleview Crested Butte, CO 81224
   970 349 5882
Doctors Garden   580 Main St #300 Carbondale, CO 81623
   970 963 9323
Green Essentials Medical LLC 404 10th St Glenwood Springs, CO
81601   970 230 9057
Green Cross Rifle 120 East 3rd St Rifle, CO 81650
   970 625 1053
Greenwerkz Glenwood Springs
   2922 South Glen Avenue #B Glenwood Springs, CO 81601
   970 366 4600
Leaf Aspen   730 E Cooper St Aspen, CO 81611
   970 920 4220
Rifle Mountain Dispensary   124 West 3rd St Rifle, CO 81650
   970 625 3359
Western Slope Caregivers   120 W 4th Rifle, CO 81650
   970 625 2040

Idaho Springs Area
Ever Green Herbal Remedies LLC
   15 Colorado Blvd Idaho Springs, CO 80452
   303 567 2706
Green Grass 440 Lawrence St Central City, CO 80427
   303 582 5088

High Country Healing III   1221 County Road 308 Downieville,
CO 80436 720 242 8692

Milagro Wellness 1181 County Road 308 Dumont, CO 80436
720 379 3672

Mountain Medicinals Wellness Center
1800 Colorado Blvd #5 Idaho Springs, CO 80452
303 567 4211

Natural Mystic Wellness Center
204 E Main St Buena Vista, CO 81211
719 395 6226

Natures Medicine Salida230 West 16th St Salida, CO 81201
719 539 3207

Serene Wellness LLC   13 East Park Ave Empire, CO 80438
303 569 2011

Sergeant Green Leaf Wellness Center
1402 Argentine St Georgetown, CO 80444
303 569 0444

Sunrise Solutions LLC   43 Main St Bailey, CO 80421
303 816 MEDS

Tenderfoot Health Collective 840 Oak St Salida, CO 81201
719 539 8661

The Annie's 135 Nevada St Central City, CO 80427
303 582 5171

The Kine Mine   2818 Colorado Blvd Idaho Springs, CO 80452
303 567 2018

Steamboat Springs Area

Craig Apothecary 611 Breeze St Craig, CO 81625
970 824 5580

Golden Leaf 1755 S Lincoln Ave Steamboat Springs, CO 80477
970 870 2941

Mary's   200 South Sharp Ave Oak Creek, CO 80467
    970 736 8212
Rocky Mountain Remedies   2750 Downhill Plaza #205
Steamboat Springs, CO 80487   970 871 2768

Durango Area
Acme Healing Center   555 South Camino Del Rio Bldg C Unit
#A1 Durango, CO 81303   970 247 2190
    Acme Healing Center   157 US Hwy 550 Ridgway, CO 81432
    970 626 4099
    Alpine Wellness   300 W Colorado Ave Telluride, CO 81435
    970 728 1834
    Animas Herbal Wellness Center
    1111 Camino Del Rio Ste 5 Durango, CO 81301
    970 385 8622
    Colo Med Center   4860 N Townsend Ave Montrose, CO 81401
    970 252 8880
    Delilah LLC   753 Vance Dr Telluride, CO 81435
    970 728 8803
    Durango Organics And Wellness Center
    72 Suttle St Unit F Durango, CO 81301
    970 259 3674
    La Casa Cannabis 205 Main St San Luis, CO 81152
    719 672 4220
    La Casa Cannabis II   5986 Budweiser Way Alamosa, CO 81101
    719 589 3503
    Natures Own Wellness Center
    927 Hwy 3 Durango, CO 81301
    970 259 0283
    Rocky Mountain High   48 County Rd 250 Unit 6 Durango, CO
81301   970 259 3714

Sante Alternative Wellness   742 ½ Main Ave Durango, CO 81301
    970 375 BUDS
Telluride Bud Company 135 S Spruce St Telluride, CO 81435
    970 239 6039
Telluride Green Room   250 South Fir Street Telluride, CO 81435
    970 728 7999
The Acceptus Group   555 Rivergate Lane #B2-135 Durango, CO
81301   970 259 1647
The Herbal Alternative 1531 Lebanon Road Cortez, CO 81321
    970 529 7007
True Earth Medicine   1104 East Main St Cortez, CO 81321
    970 565 6500

Breckenridge Area
Alma Cannabis Therapeutics 447 N Main St Alma, CO 80420
    719 839 0109
AlpenGlow Botanicals   1805 Airport Rd #B1C Breckenridge, CO
80424   970 389 6839
Breckenridge Cannabis Club 226 South Main Street Breckenridge,
CO 80424 970 453 4900
Breckenridge Organic Therapy
    1900 Airport Rd Ste A1 Breckenridge, CO 80424
    970 453 0420
Cloud City Compassionate Care
    1013 Poplar St Leadville, CO 80461
    719 486 4013
High Country Healing   191 Blue River Parkway Silverthorne, CO
80498   970 468 7858
High Country Healing II 40 S Main St Alma, CO 80420
    719 836 9000
Holistic Healthcare   0105 Edwards Village Blvd Ste E202

Edwards, CO 81632 970 926 4221

Medical Marijuana Of The Rockies

720 Summit Blvd Ste 101A Frisco, CO 80443

970 668 MEDS

Natures Spirit   113 E 7th St Leadville, CO 80461

719 486 1900

New Hope Wellness Center   210 Edwards Village B110 Edwards, CO 81632 970 569 3701

Organix   1795 Airport Rd Unit A2 Breckenridge, CO 80424

970 453 1340

Rocky Mountain High   105 Edwards Village Blvd Unit C104 Edwards, CO 81632 970 926 4408

Soulshine Medical Consulting

1805 Airport Rd Ste B2B Breckenridge, CO 80424

970 453 7685

SweetLeaf Pioneer 1286 Chambers Ste #105 Eagle, CO 81631

970 328 9060

Tree Line Premier MMC 40801 US 6 Ste #5 Eagle-Vail, CO 81620

970 949 1887

California

Los Angeles Area

215 Caregivers   3119 N Main St Los Angeles, CA 90031
   323 227 5874

35 Cap Olive Caregiver 1400 S Olive Los Angeles, CA 90015
   213 746 4258

3rd Street Caregivers   3809 W 3rd St Los Angeles, CA 90020
   213 427 1234

420 Collective   12421 Venice Blvd #4 Los Angeles, CA 90066
   310 401 3454

4THC   3459 East 4th St Los Angeles, CA 90063
   323 545 2020

A #1   8777 W Pico Blvd West Los Angeles, CA 90035
   310 271 2669

A Downtown Holistic Center 1160 Glendale Blvd Los Angeles, CA
90026   213 787 3101

AA Caregivers   5081 W Pico Blvd Los Angeles, CA 90019
   323 424 7867

Aardvarks   5597 W Pico Blvd Los Angeles, CA 90019
   323 424 4754

Absolute Herbal   2201 S San Pedro St Unit #B Los Angeles, CA 90011   213 765 9550

Alcam Medical Delivery Delivery
562 547 2308

All Better Collective   435 E Vernon Ave Los Angeles, CA 90011
323 718 2547

Alpine Caregivers 6134 Pico Blvd Los Angeles, CA 90035
323 424 4839

Alternative Institute For Relief
8626 S Figueroa Ave Los Angeles, CA 90003
323 984 4272

Alternative Relief Institute   1855 W Manchester Ave #105 Los Angeles, CA 90047   323 751 3049

AMG   1715 E Alondra Blvd Compton, CA 90221
310 617 5760

Artists Collective Delivery   323 979 7822

Bayside Patients   1801 N Long Beach Blvd Compton, CA 90221
424 785 6239

BCS   6333 S Broadway Los Angeles, CA 90003
323 778 8080

Beach Center 310 Culver Blvd Playa Del Rey, CA 90293
310 821 4420

Beachside Collective   1325 Venice Blvd Venice, CA 90291
424 500 2312

Bellflower Patients Group   16203 Clark Ave Unit E Bellflower, CA 90706 562 412 5442

Best Buds Delivery Delivery   310 351 5449

Best Meds Delivery   Delivery
310 363 3068

Best On Venice   4912 Venice Blvd Los Angeles, CA 90019
323 879 9049

Beverly Hills Dollatella   11906 Wilshire Blvd #6 Brentwood, CA 90025   424 832 7543

BHP Group   3615 E 8th St Los Angeles, CA 90023
323 980 9585

BHPC   1812 North Broadway East Los Angeles, CA 90031
323 405 3755

Breathe Easy Wellness Delivery
Delivery   213 435 8429

Broadway Organic Center   8109 S Broadway Los Angeles, CA 90003   323 920 4429

Cal Med   754 W Washinton Blvd Marina Del Rey, CA 90292
310 747 4795

Cali's Finest Compassionate 8540 Venice Blvd Los Angeles, CA 90034   310 838 5800

California Alternative Caregivers
122 Lincoln Blvd #204 Venice, CA 90291
877 219 3809

California Caregivers Alliance
2815 W Sunset Blvd #201 Los Angeles, CA 90026
213 353 0100

California Healing Gardens   2501 Lincoln Blvd Venice, CA 90291
310 822 4420

California Herbal Remedies   5470 Valley Blvd Los Angeles, CA 90032   323 342 9110

CalTrees   Delivery   530 748 5118

Canna Couture   717 S Long Beach Blvd Compton, CA 90221
424 288 0922

Cannacierge Delivery   818 693 6060

CCC Delivery Delivery   562 215 2398

CCC LA 9459 South Normandie Ave Los Angeles, CA 90044
323 418 8400

Central Remedies 5712 S Central Ave Los Angeles, CA 90011
    323 231 9700
China Inn   812 Lincoln Blvd Venice, CA 90291
    323 703 8645
Chronic Care Medical   4902 South Vermont Los Angeles, CA
90037
Chronicpractor Caregiver   5751 W Adams Blvd Los Angeles, CA
90016   323 592 3511
City Compassionate Caregivers
    606 E 4th St Los Angeles, CA 90013
    213 935 8996
City Of Angels Healing Center
    100 West 17th #29 Los Angeles, CA 90015
    213 745 7760
Clean Green 8338 Lincoln Blvd Los Angeles, CA 90045
    310 421 1446
Clone Queen Genetics 1619 Los Angeles St Los Angeles, CA
90015   424 209 7746
Clover American Life   8533 Washington Blvd Culver, City CA
90232   323 691 2794
Club Oro   1314 Venice Blvd Los Angeles, CA 90006
    424 265 9666
Club Venice 1711 Pacific Ave Venice, CA 90291
    310 359 5002
Coastal Reef Delivery   818 675 8706
Community Wellness Association
    12041 Wilshire Blvd #1 Los Angeles, CA 90025
    877 292 4242
Compton Flight Club   325 W Compton Blvd Compton, CA 90220
    424 232 7988
CR Medical Crenshaw Wax House

4114 Crenshaw Blvd Los Angeles, CA 90008

323 348 4015

Crazy Grass Collective   3724 W Sunset Blvd Los Angeles, CA 90026   213 327 4466

Crenshaw Caregivers Inc   7621 Crenshaw Blvd Los Angeles, CA 90043 323 758 8078

Culver City Collective   10887 Venice Blvd Ste A Los Angeles, CA 90034   310 838 5888

CWC   5830 Bonsallo Ave Los Angeles, CA 90044

323 696 9344

Daily Dabs Wax Bar   3231 N Main St East Los Angeles, CA 90031   323 671 8129

Dank Door Delivery   Delivery

562 758 5332

Dank Medical   Delivery   562 322 8131

DDD Caregivers Inc   328 South Alvarado St Los Angeles, CA 90057   213 924 7649

DHC DeliveryDelivery   213 787 3101

DinoBud   Delivery   855 346 6283

Discount Bud Shop   114 E 12th St Los Angeles, CA 90015

213 493 6500

DNPM   4902 W Pico Blvd 2nd Floor Los Angeles, CA 90019

323 455 4903

Downtown Care   404 West Cesar E Chavez Los Angeles, CA 90012   213 999 9014

Downtown Discount Center   1123 West 7th St #B Los Angeles, CA 90017   213 488 2904

Downtown NaturalDelivery   213 949 1353

Downtown Natural Caregivers

312 S Wall St Los Angeles, CA 90013

213 625 0301

Dr Greenthumb   2221 S Main Los Angeles, CA 90007
213 747 2620
Drive420.com   Delivery   310 289 7174
DTHC Lounge   1400 S Alameda St Los Angeles, CA 90021
213 765 4990
Earth Green Mile   2679 E Florence Ave Huntington Park, CA
90255   323 835 6940
Earth's Way To Relief   243 West Florence Ave Los Angeles, CA
90003   323 215 5964
Eden Wellness Collective   11924 W Jefferson Blvd West Los
Angeles, CA 90230   310 397 5700
Emerald Garden Delivery   Delivery
213 841 5991
Euphoric   10655 West Pico Blvd Los Angeles, CA 90064
310 446 8100
Field Of Greens   5226 Pico Blvd Los Angeles, CA 90019
323 424 3050
Figueroa Patients Association
8814 Figueroa St Los Angeles, CA 90003
323 758 5060
Florence Green Garden 2050 W Florence Los Angeles, CA 90047
818 621 8366
Fruit Of Life Delivery   Delivery
310 402 7005
FWB Clones   Delivery   818 271 1089
G West 1901 Rodeo Rd Los Angeles, CA 90018
323 290 9250
Garden Gateway   Delivery   888 315 4679
GEC   2100 South Santa Fe Ave Compton, CA 90221
310 605 0600
GGR   2000 Cotner Ave West Los Angeles, CA 90025

310 473 3509

GGR   Delivery   310 905 2086

GMC Inc   4817 South Normandie Ave Los Angeles, CA 90037
323 292 4568

GMC Inc   847 W Florence Los Angeles, CA 90044
323 759 9697

Gold Collective   2034 W Wasington Ave Los Angeles, CA 90018
323 813 1212

GOTOS 8561 Broadway Los Angeles, CA 90003
323 786 4755

GPC   1101 S Robertson Blvd Ste #104 Los Angeles, CA 90035
310 550 6993

Grateful Meds   516 E 4th St Los Angeles, CA 90013
213 613 1288

Green Birds   2645 Crenshaw Blvd Los Angeles, CA 90016
424 703 3420

Green Cure Venice1716 Main St Venice, CA 90291
310 306 5511

Green Goddess Collective   70 Windward Ave Venice, CA 90291
310 396 7770

Green Leaf Collective   Delivery
888 815 2453

Green Light   Delivery   424 888 4204

Green Light Delivery   Delivery
424 888 4204

Green Magic Delivery   Delivery
323 557 3149

Green Miracle Healing Delivery
Delivery   818 232 8684

Green Shield Delivery   TheGreenShield.Org – Delivery

Green Street Wellness Center 6218D Manchester Ave Los Angeles, CA 90045 855 420 0215

Green Temple   1651 West Temple St Los Angeles, CA 90026
323 432 7391

Green Wave 7815 S Western Ave Los Angeles, CA 90047
323 750 2600

Greenbike   Delivery   855 476 2453

Greener By Nature 11919 Wilshire Blvd West Los Angeles, CA 90025   323 515 4400

GreenLightMeds.Com   Delivery
424 253 KUSH

Greens R Us 814 S Vermont Ave Los Angeles, CA 90005
213 739 9201

H And H Coop   1938 West Adams Blvd Los Angeles, CA 90018
323 733 0442

Harmony HC 2501 Sunset Blvd #C Los Angeles, CA 90026
213 529 4647

HDB Medical Delivery Services
Delivery   562 457 0419

Healing Haze 5779 Venice Blvd Culver City, CA 90019
323 692 7419

Healthy Herbal Care Plus   313 North Virgil Ave Los Angeles, CA 90004 323 660 0386

Heaven On Earth 2743 S Robertson Blvd Los Angeles, CA 90034
310 339 1105

Herbalcure Cooperative 11318 West Pico Blvd Los Angeles, CA 90064   310 312 5215

Herban Delivery   Delivery   213 327 6145

Herbman   3808 S Western Ave Los Angeles, CA 90062
323 373 0589

Highest Quality Solutions   1575 Westwood Blvd #302 Los

Angeles, CA 90024   424 832 3652
   HMC Premier Medical Delivery
      Delivery   805 910 5523
   Hollywood Holistic   1543 Sawtelle Blvd, Los Angeles, CA
90025   424 256 2554
   Hot Zone Medical 1612 S Hill St Los Angeles, CA 90015
      213 765 6099
   House Of Dank   2253 W Pico Blvd Los Angeles, CA 90006
      213 252 8220
   IGPA   Delivery   310 941 1029
   Indiana Caregivers Inc   3816 E Olympic Blvd Los Angeles, CA
90023   323 264 7200
   Infinity Healing Center 4512 ½ W Pico Blvd Los Angeles, CA
90019   323 692 0048
   IW 611 E Imperial Hwy Suite 107 Los Angeles, CA 90059

   JJ Herbal   12249 Santa Monica Blvd Los Angeles, CA 90025
      310 979 3816
   Kellys Collective   8638 W Pico Blvd Los Angeles, CA 90035
      310 854 5874
   Kind For Cures   9850 Exposition Blvd Los Angeles, CA 90034
      310 836 5463
   Kush Collective   1111 S La Brea Blvd Los Angeles, CA 90019
      323 938 5874
   La Brea Caregivers 1188 S La Brea Ave Los Angeles, CA 90019
      323 549 0400
   La Brea Collective 5057 W Pico Blvd Los Angeles, CA 90019
      323 424 3908
   La Cienega Caregivers   1551 La Cienega Blvd West Los Angeles,
CA 90035 424 249 3531
   LA Meds 4 Less   1720 East 14th St #A Los Angeles, CA 90021

213 744 9474

LA Treehouse   756 Washington Blvd Marina Del Rey, CA 90292   310 577 8030

LACC   1403 S Hill St Los Angeles, CA 90015
213 572 7199

Lakewood Elite Medicinal   Delivery
562 280 8599

LAXCC 8332 Lincoln Blvd Los Angeles, CA 90045
310 439 9176

Main St Caregivers 103 E 5th St Los Angeles, CA 90013
213 258 2168

Manchester Caregivers 1425 W Manchester Ave Suite C Los Angeles, CA 90047   323 758 8610

Mecca Natural Medicine 5650 W Washington Blvd Los Angeles, CA 90016   323 937 0299

Medcity 5140 W Washington Blvd Los Angeles, CA 90016
323 939 0001

Medicure   5135 Alhambra Ave Los Angeles, CA 90032
818 437 5402

Medstar   1155 S Robertson Blvd Los Angeles, CA 90035
310 385 5680

Miracle High Mile Inc   Delivery
310 870 1818

Mr Nice Guy Delivery   Delivery
323 639 0185

Mr Nice Guy Wax Bar   1126 S Los Angeles St Unit B Los Angeles, CA 90015 213 273 4543

Nature Cann Delivery   Delivery
562 209 6704

Nature's Wonder Caregivers Group Inc
1330 W Olympic Blvd Los Angeles, CA 90015

213 380 5874

Natures Choice Direct   Delivery

562 446 0494

Natures Cure Inc   5300 W Century Blvd Ste 124 Los Angeles, CA 90045   310 645 0173

Natures Way Delivery   Delivery

855 929 2278

New Era   1238 S Flower St Los Angeles, CA 90015

213 747 7969

Next Door Wellness   1443 Jefferson Los Angeles, CA 90007

323 733 4420

NGHC   8501 S Fiueroa St Los Angeles, CA 90003

562 388 5204

NNCC   9021 Exposition Blvd Los Angeles, CA 90034

310 202 NNCC

NTSD   609 N Long Beach Blvd Compton, CA 90221

310 941 7109

NWA   10717 S Central Ave #1 Los Angeles, CA 90059

424 221 2023

OC Herbal Care   Delivery   213 284 2631

Oceanside Collective   1107 S Alvarado St Los Angeles, CA 90006   213 382 1981

OG Collective   4520 S Broadway St Los Angeles, CA 90037

323 500 9977

OG Green Bear   106 E 17th St #11 Los Angles, CA 90015

213 273 3802

OGK Holistic 1514 N Long Beach Blvd Unit D Compton, CA 90221

310 415 7414

One Love Herbal   8940 National Blvd West Los Angeles, CA 90034   310 558 9333

One Stop Shop   5901 Whittier Blvd Unit D Los Angeles, CA

90022   323 313 9148

Organic Caregivers   2249 Westwood Blvd Unit A Los Angeles, CA 90064 310 270 2482

Organic Green Club Inc 1260 S Soto St Los Angeles, CA 90023   323 526 9848

Organic Medicine 111 E 9th St Los Angeles, CA 90015   213 236 0848

Organics Herbal Nutrition Center
1435 S La Cienega Blvd Los Angeles, CA 90035
310 657 4148

Palliative Healing Centers   1122 Maple Ave #205 Los Angeles, CA 90015 213 741 1914

Pazaliko Collective   1107 S Robertson Blvd Los Angeles, CA 90035   747 444 8488

People's Choice   2840 E Olympic Blvd #D Los Angeles, CA 90023   323 718 5308

Pico Patient Wellness   2273 W Pico Blvd Los Angeles, CA 90006   213 674 7388

Platinum Club   2617 E Cesar Chavez Los Angeles, CA 90033   323 303 4420

Pot Spot Collective   900 S Westmoreland Ave Ste 102 Los Angeles, CA 90006   213 381 9991

Precision Medical Caregivers 3913 W 6th St Los Angeles, CA 90020   213 382 7971

Purelife Alternative Wellness Center
1649 S La Cienega Blvd Los Angeles, CA 90035
310 246 9345

Purple Heart Compassion   5823 Pico Blvd Los Angeles, CA 90019   323 272 4392

Purple Leaf   4182 S Western Ave Los Angeles, CA 90062   323 299 5323

Red Eye Society   737 S Vermont Ave Los Angeles, CA 90005
   213 381 3420
Red Night   1804 S La Cienega Blvd Los Angeles, CA 90035
   747 800 7788
Riddlers   11508 W Pico Blvd Los Angeles, CA 90064
   310 717 7482
SC Delivery   Delivery   310 905 2733
SCWC   6002 South Broadway Ave Los Angeles, CA 90003
   323 750 5550
Secret Gardens Delivery LA   Delivery
   323 230 9500
Shareluck   1804 N Broadway Los Angeles, CA 90031
   323 551 5874
SL Caregivers   1126 S Western Ave Los Angeles, CA 90006
   323 733 1700
Smokers Delight LAX   5710 Manchester Ave Ste 203 Los
Angeles, CA 90045   310 568 9602
Soto St Compassionate 1300 South Soto St Los Angeles, CA
90023   323 264 3018
South Central Caregivers   1136 E Imperial Hwy Watts, CA
90059 Watts, CA 90059   213 341 0407
South Gate Elite Medicinal   Delivery
   323 425 1601
Southern California Care Collective
   2270 Venice Blvd Los Angeles, CA 90006
   323 731 1880
Southern Pacific Healing   522 S Lorena St Los Angeles, CA
90063   323 354 4182
Sowa   2805 E Washington Blvd Los Angeles, CA 90023
   323 881 0707
Spectrum   3567 W 3rd St Los Angeles, CA 90020

213 273 3764

Spring Mountain   Delivery   323 540 2971

Sticky Delivery   Delivery   310 237 8803

Tha Dank Bank   Delivery   562 310 6298

The 710 Club Delivery Delivery
    310 227 2096

The Collective Center   521 S Alvarado St Los Angeles, CA 90057
    213 949 2675

The Dank Bank   Delivery   562 310 6298

The Dragon Collective 3977 West 6th St Los Angeles, CA 90020
    213 529 4016

The Exquisite Flower   2010 W Pico Blvd #2 Los Angeles, CA
90006   213 389 9987

The Farmacy Venice   1509 Abbot Kinney Venice, CA 90291
    310 392 3890

The Goddess Delivers   Delivery
    855 426 5246

The Green Guys   Delivery   323 331 2361

The Greenfellas   4426 ½ Avalon Blvd Los Angeles, CA 90011
    323 231 0111

The Hemp Garden 3787 E Olympic Blvd Los Angeles, CA 90023
    323 260 4840

The Hempery   4700 S Hoover St Los Angeles, CA 90037

Top Flight   Delivery   310 363 3068

Topshelf Wellness Delivery   Delivery
    855 893 9965

TQ Healing   2623 W Sunset Blvd Silverlake/Echo Park, CA 90026
    213 973 6369

Tribal House Care 1105 W 23rd St Los Angeles, CA 90007
    213 258 6233

Trinity Holistic Caregivers   131 E 3rd St Los Angeles, CA 90013

213 253 4733

True Help Center 4331 Crenshaw Blvd Los Angeles, CA 90008
310 703 7939

Universal Holistic Collective   1709 W Vernon Ave Los Angeles, CA
90062   323 290 1006

Unseen Green   Delivery   562 343 3016

Valley Herbal 6620 Crenshaw Blvd Los Angeles, CA 90043
818 800 9968

Venice Alternative 421 Rose Ave Venice, CA 90291
424 238 5491

Venice Beach Care Center   410 Lincoln Blvd Venice, CA 90291
310 399 4307

Venice Blvd Patients Association
8535 Venice Blvd Los Angeles, CA 90034
310 204 2200

Venice Caregivers 8543 Venice Blvd Los Angeles, CA 90034
310 873 3310

Venice Collective   12581 Venice Blvd Ste 201 Los Angeles, CA
90066   310 437 0308

Venice Medical Center 9636 Venice Blvd Suite A West Los
Angeles, CA 90232 424 603 2133

Venice Organics   724 Lincoln Blvd Los Angeles, CA 90291
310 450 3200

VHC   955 S Vermont Ave #P 2nd Floor Los Angeles, CA 90006
213 388 9990

VHC Club   10955 Venice Blvd Los Angeles, CA 90034
310 837 5100

VIP OG Private Delivery Delivery
323 568 7755

WDC   2191 Whittier Blvd East Los Angeles, CA 90023
323 265 2265

West Adams 1   1662 ½ W Adams Blvd Los Angeles, CA 90007
323 230 9500

Western Compassion Collective
7509 S Western Ave Los Angeles, CA 90047
323 759 7509

Western Discount Center   1570 S Western Ave #102 Los
Angeles, CA 90006   323 733 2913

Western Patient Group   9107 South Western Ave Los Angeles, CA
90047   818 572 7947

Western Therapeutic Collective
447 S Western Ave Los Angeles, CA 90020
213 381 5209

Westlake Collective   1675 W 11th St Los Angeles, CA 90015
424 777 8099

Westside Care Givers   2370 S Robertson Blvd Los Angeles, CA
90034   310 558 0190

Westside Holistic Remedy   2346 Westwood Blvd Ste 1 Los
Angeles, CA 90064   310 441 2800

Westside Organic Delivery   Delivery
310 309 9752

Westwood Village Collective   10966 Le Conte Ave Westwood, CA
90024   310 208 4254

WHC   3518 Whittier Blvd Los Angeles, CA 90023
323 475 4888

World Peace Caregivers 4713 West Washington Blvd Los Angeles,
CA 90016 323 200 3777

WWC   8911 S Western Ave Los Angeles, CA 90047
323 455 3867

WWMG 420   1882 S Western Ave Los Angeles, CA 90006
323 373 9456

Yakwu Corporation   Delivery

323 989 4588

Yolo 'Bogo' Collective   1200 South Main St Los Angeles, CA 90015   323 424 2971

Your Choice Collective 5404 Alhambra Ave Los Angeles, CA 90032   626 502 0343

Long Beach Area

1 Love Beach Club Delivery   562 343 5388

5 Diamond Quality Collective Delivery
    714 822 7856

ABC Delivery Delivery   562 826 2052

All Patients Delivery   Delivery
    562 719 3742

Avalon C   814 N Avalon Blvd Wilmington, CA 90744
    310 835 1127

BeachCitiesMarijuana.Com   Delivery
    310 894 6337

Canna Quick Delivery   562 743 5557

Caregivers Express   Delivery
    562 326 7056

Cornerstone Delivery   562 213 0057

Daily Deals   522 W 9th St San Pedro, CA 90731
    424 224 2294

Dank Medical   Delivery   562 322 8131

DPG   2016 E Anaheim St Long Beach, CA 90813
    562 433 9000

Fullerton Flowers Delivery   714 757 2392

Green Dove Co-Operative   408 North Avalon Blvd Wilmington, CA 90744 310 830 0834

Green Tiger Delivery   Delivery
    562 235 8185

Greenmart   910 West Pacific Coast Hwy Wilmington, CA 90744
    424 703 3111
Happy Meds Delivery   714 584 8471
Healing Tree Holistic Association
    Delivery   562 308 6279
LA Collective 728 N Avalon Blvd, Wilmington, CA 90744
    310 684 1066
Local 420 Patients Collective 600 S Pacific Ave #104 San Pedro,
CA 90731 310 732 1617
Locals Choice Delivery Delivery
    714 644 0385
Long Beach Specialty Health Delivery
    562 218 1340
Mary Couture Delivery Service
    Delivery   310 920 0136
Natural Green Healing   320 S Gaffey San Pedro, CA 90731
Natural Naturopathic Care   Delivery
    323 952 8348
NatureCann 4332 Atlantic Ave Long Beach, CA 90807
    323 515 4500
Natures Choice Direct   Delivery
    562 446 0494
NWCG   1111 S Pacific Ave San Pedro, CA 90731
    310 514 9665
PCH Caregivers   1418 E Pacific Coast Hwy Wilmington, CA
90744   310 830 1540
Peace Of Green   25103 Vermont Ave Harbor City, CA 90710
    310 986 8298
PR Collective 136 S Gaffey St San Pedro, CA 90731
    310 832 2420
PR Collective Mobile   Delivery

310 529 4434

Rapid Relief Delivery   562 455 3438

Shoreline   Delivery   562 235 5702

Skippy Hotbox And Wax House

   571 W 6th Street San Pedro, CA 90731

   714 591 3088

SPAS   1722 S Gaffey St San Pedro, CA 90731

   424 772 1495

TCC   1085 Redondo Long Beach, CA 90804

   562 290 9413

The Canna Delivery   Delivery

   714 429 6045

The Humble Collective Delivery

   Delivery   562 217 2146

Tree Life Collective   Delivery

   562 612 5144

Vape Dank   Delivery   562 208 3127

VIP   424 N Avalon Blvd Wilmington, CA 90744

   310 803 3338

Westcoast CC Delivery   Delivery

   310 514 6996

Wilmington Wholesale   1037 E Pacific Coast Hwy Wilmington, CA 90744   714 760 3483

Torrance Area

4G   1311 West 228 St Torrance, CA 90501

   323 319 8133

Along Came Mary Delivery   323 326 9150

BeachCitiesMarijuana.Com   Delivery

   310 894 6337

Canna Beach Delivery   Delivery

424 225 1995

Canna Hut Delivery   Delivery
   310 245 0299

CHC   1609 Lockness Place Torrance, CA 90501
   310 891 2223

Coast310   Delivery   310 730 9049

Fast And Friendly Delivery   310 870 7115

Green Bay   Delivery   626 421 3167

HSC   23700 S Western Ave Torrance, CA 90710
   310 755 9999

Manahattan Beach 420 Delivery
   310 359 9662

MarijuanaDelivery.Com Delivery
   310 272 9726

MarijuanaMarket.Com   Delivery
   310 272 9726

SBCC   1555 W Sepulveda Blvd Suite J Torrance, CA 90501
   310 517 0420

SBH Delivery Delivery   323 312 4749

SBQPG Delivery   323 451 2987

SCPA   844 W Gardena Blvd, Gardena, CA 90247
   323 544 7747

South Bay Farms   Delivery   310 755 0600

Speed Weed Delivery   888 860 8472

Spring Health House   2150 Redondo Beach Blvd Torrance, CA 90504   323 671 6695

Lancaster Area

Advanced Genetics   Delivery
   661 524 0800

All Green Collective   2753 Diamond St Rosamond, CA 93560

661 256 6493

Antelope Valley Diamond Collective

   1733 Sierra Hwy Rosamond, CA 93560

   661 256 7753

Big O Relief   Delivery   661 540 3806

Clone Queen 1841 W Ave Ste Ste K1 Lancaster, CA 93534

   424 209 7746

Evergreen Health Alliance   Delivery

   661 722 4400

From The HeavensDelivery   661 434 3317

Green Diamond Delivery Service Inc

   Delivery   661 940 1122

Green Door Organics Inc Delivery

   Delivery   661 769 6337

Green Express   Delivery   661 524 5111

Happy Medical Delivery Delivery

   661 537 4331

Higher Planning Group Delivery

   661 400 7738

Hwy 138 Collective   13120b Pearblossom Hwy Pearblossom,
CA 93553 661 944 9140

   Indoor Delivery   Delivery   818 582 0267

   Littlerock Big Stoned Delivery

      Delivery   661 269 3125

   Meds Direct Delivery   661 480 8858

   One Stop Healers Delivery   818 821 9859

   Organic Health Solutions   1315 W Rosamond Blvd Suite 1A
Rosamond, CA 93560   661 256 0220

   Queen's Botanica 7606 Pearblossom Hwy Little Rock, CA 93543

      661 547 9137

   The Green Medics Delivery   661 233 4890

West Coast Delivery   Delivery
    661 209 8794

West Covina Area
4040 Collective   Delivery   626 328 9513
626 Kush   Delivery   626 626 5874
7 Wonders   Delivery   714 616 0437
Acme Silver Place   1261 S Hacienda Blvd Hacienda Heights, CA
91745   626 330 3121
Best Budz   146 E Bonita Ave San Dimas, CA 91773
    626 388 8271
Best Choice Deliveries   Delivery
    626 923 0682
Brisk Delivery   Delivery   626 923 7121
Cali Green Care And Wellness
    Delivery   818 390 2333
Chronic Care Collective Delivery
    626 581 6355
CMC Medical Delivery Services
    Delivery   714 294 6273
CMG   Delivery   626 963 2628
CMS   Delivery   818 454 4328
Cowboy ClubDelivery   909 730 9313
Dank Dabs Delivery Diamond Bar
    Delivery   951 543 7283
Direct Connect   Delivery   626 343 0314
DM   Delivery   888 776 1136
Friendly Xpress   Delivery   562 325 4435
Good Leaf Collective   Delivery
    888 815 2453
Green Coast Deliveries Delivery

888 235 9771

Green Cross Holistic   Delivery
909 568 1815

Green District Delivery Services
Delivery   626 696 9398

Green Era Collective   Delivery
626 423 2405

Green Rush Delivery   Delivery
626 782 3270

HDB Medical Delivery Service Delivery
562 457 0419

High Society Collective Delivery
626 215 5045

House Of Wax   Delivery   626 551 1127

Kush Connection Delivery   626 415 4150

LABRATS   Delivery   323 973 8090

Mercurys Flight   Delivery   626 409 7840

Organics Finest   Delivery   626 720 1513

Releaf Central   Delivery   818 929 6045

Relief Green Wheels   Delivery
562 587 2258

Route 66 Delivery Inc   Delivery
626 230 9412

SGV Compassion Delivery   626 383 5524

SGV Med Express Delivery   626 200 3587

The Dab Connection   Delivery
909 979 1207

The Honor Roll Collective   Delivery
626 277 1921

Unseen Green   Delivery   562 343 3016

Valas Collective Care   Delivery

626 393 9640

Vega Meats Patients Association
   15835 Gale Ave Hacienda Heights, CA 91745
   626 417 7766

Glendale/Pasadena Area

AHC   Delivery   323 695 9628

Alternative Solution Delivery Delivery
   626 841 2747

Blue Sky   Delivery   818 640 2196

Emerald Bliss Medical Marijuana
   Delivery   888 809 2797

Green 2 Go   Delivery   626 421 3167

Green Earth Delivery   Delivery
   323 982 9042

MCC   44 North Mentor Ave Pasadena, CA 91106
   626 744 3191

One Stop Healers Delivery   818 821 9859

Organics Finest   Delivery   626 720 1513

Quality Green   Delivery   626 421 3167

The Blue Diamond Center Delivery
   Delivery   818 749 2444

WCC   Delivery   310 905 9126

Whittier Area

3P Delivery   Delivery   562 686 5270

CBN Collective   Delivery   562 338 1256

Dank Door Delivery   Delivery
   562 758 5332

Friends And Family QPA   Delivery
   562 325 1836

HDB Medical Delivery Service Delivery
  562 457 0419
OC Farmacy Delivery   800 420 6935
The Canna Delivery   Delivery
  714 429 6045

Tujunga/Sun Valley Area
7006 Collective   7006 Foothill Blvd Tujunga, CA 91042
  818 951 9991
Alternameds Sunland   8517 Foothill Blvd Sunland, CA 91040
  818 951 4555
Bestocare   E 7469 Foothill Blvd #B Tujunga, CA 91042
  818 951 1368
Blue Sky   8233 San Fernando Rd Sun Valley, CA 91352
  818 640 2196
Exotic Buds   11354 Saticoy St Sun Valley, CA 91352
  818 720 6998
Foothill Wellness Center   7132 Foothill Blvd Tujunga, CA
91042   818 352 3388
  Green Life Caregivers   7108 Foothill Blvd Tujunga, CA 91042
  818 273 4205
HMC   8423 San Fernando Rd #C Sun Valley, CA 91352
  818 924 2222
One Stop Healers Delivery   818 821 9859
SVC   11000 Randall St #E Sun Valley, CA 91352
  818 504 2661
Sylmar Caregivers Inc   9960 Glenoaks Blvd Unit A Sun Valley, CA
91352   818 768 2817
  The Little Cottage Caregivers 8133 Foothill Blvd Sunland, CA
91040   818 352 3730

Ventura Area

360   Delivery   818 297 2199
California ConnoisseursDelivery
   805 225 4415
Club 215   Delivery   805 402 5955
Garden Gateway   Delivery   888 315 4679
Green Cuisine Delivery Delivery
   805 705 4993
Green Garden Health   Delivery
   805 296 0399
H2H Collective   Delivery   323 391 4631
HDHT's Green Tree   Delivery
   805 620 8508
Medicann.org   Delivery   860 469 5874
On Deck Coop   Delivery   818 253 4632
Organic Remedy Connection Delivery
   805 328 5171
Top Notch Hydroponic Delivery
   661 645 0734
VC Kush Co-Op   Delivery   805 208 9994
Ventura Collective Delivery   818 540 6120

Hollywood Area

215 Collective   4534 Fountain Ave Hollywood, CA 90029
   323 669 1885
7411 Lankershim 7411 Lankershim Blvd North Hollywood, CA
91605   818 764 1203
A1 Organic Collective   10540 Victory Blvd North Hollywood, CA
91606   818 508 2400
Alternative Med Center 5100 Lankershim Blvd North Hollywood,
CA 91601 818 508 6024

Associated Patients Collective
10714 ¼ Riverside Drive Toluca Lake, CA 91602
818 761 1557
B52 Organic Healing   10651 Burbank Blvd North Hollywood, CA
91601   818 506 4420
Best Choice   1002 N Vermont Ave Los Angeles, CA 90029
323 665 5712
Black Rose Collective   7262 Melrose Ave Los Angeles, CA 90046
323 932 1244
Bud Stop   12439 Victory Blvd North Hollywood, CA 91606
818 200 6792
Buddha Bar Collective   440 ½ N La Cienega Blvd West Hollywood,
CA 90048 310 657 4202
Budelicious   6423 Selma Ave Los Angeles, CA 90028
323 960 8281
California Compassionate   4720 Vineland Ave North Hollywood,
CA 91602 818 980 6337
California Herbal Healing Center
1437 N La Brea Ave Los Angles, CA 90028
877 420 5874
California Natural Collective 744 N La Brea Ave Hollywood, CA
90038   323 939 9111
California Patients Alliance   8271 Melrose Ave #102 West
Hollywood, CA 90046   323 655 1735
Canna LA   5205 Agnes Ave Valley Village, CA 91607
800 865 2427
Canna Medics   6325 Lankershim Blvd North Hollywood, CA
91606   818 509 9200
CCF   2332 Fletcher Dr Hollywood, CA 90039
323 666 2332
CCSC Collective   7324 Melrose Ave Los Angeles, CA 90046

323 930 0550

City Of Angels   4877 Melrose Ave Hollywood, CA 90029
323 464 2222

Cure Herbal Collective 10704 Vanowen St North Hollywood, CA
91605   818 691 3571

Cure With Herbs Inc   5235 Melrose Ave Los Angeles, CA 90038
323 468 8330

DCC   5430 Cahuenga Blvd North Hollywood, CA 91601
818 303 6666

Divine Wellness Center 5056 Lankershim Blvd North Hollywood,
CA 91601 818 508 9948

Dr Green Meds   4741 Laurel Canyon Blvd Ste 101 Valley Village,
CA 91607 818 985 4020

Dr Greenthumbs   6645 Lankershim Blvd North Hollywood, CA
91606   818 765 WEED

Eden Therapy Collective   6757 ½ Santa Monica Blvd Los
Angeles, CA 90038   323 463 8937

Elevation Wellness 13122 Sherman Way North Hollywood, CA
91605   818 765 5933

EME Medical 4008 W 3rd St Hollywood, CA 90020
323 454 0505

Fountain Of Wellbeing   7231 Hinds Ave North Hollywood, CA
91605   818 982 7420

Fresh CP   11178 Burbank Blvd North Hollywood, CA 91601
818 985 1994

Friendly Meds   5415 Santa Monica Blvd Hollywood, CA 90029
323 229 6127

FWB Clones Delivery   818 271 1089

FWB Delivery Delivery   818 982 7420

Good Karma 1119 North Hudson Ave Hollywood, CA 90038
323 464 6404

GoodnessDelivered.Org Delivery
   818 452 6609
Green Kiss Collective   6356 Vineland Ave North Hollywood, CA
91606   818 732 7272
Green Miracle Healing   7503 Laurel Canyon Blvd North
Hollywood, CA 91605   818 232 8684
Green Palace 3615 Beverly Blvd Los Angeles, CA 90004
   424 230 2220
Green Spot   12517 Oxnard St North Hollywood, CA 91606
   818 761 3100
Greenhouse Herbal Center LLC
   5224 Hollywood Blvd Los Angeles, CA 90027
   323 666 2591
GreenLightMeds.Com   Delivery
   4254 253 5874
GS Caregivers   6025 Santa Monica Blvd Hollywood, CA 90038
   323 465 5570
GTC   7561 Lankershim Blvd Ste 104 North Hollywood, CA
91605   8118 505 3181
HCMA   10929 Vanowen St Unit A North Hollywood, CA 91605
   818 538 4262
Hezekiah Incorporated 1606 N Gower St Hollywood, CA 90028
   323 467 6484
HHM Delivery   Delivery   323 835 5037
Hillhurst Meds   1757 Hillhurst Ave Los Angeles, CA 90027
   323 913 9096
Hollyweed   1607 N El Centro Ave #24 2nd Floor Hollywood, CA
90028   323 469 9873
Hollywood Caregivers Express
   Delivery   424 266 0029
Hollywood Hills Collective   3324 Barham Blvd Los Angeles, CA

90068   323 380 6207

Hollywood Holistics   4719 Melrose Ave Hollywood, CA 90029
323 522 6469

Hollywood Meds   Delivery   310 310 1891

Hollywood THC   5322 Sunset Blvd 2nd Floor Los Angeles, CA
90027   323 465 9513

HTC   12410 Burbank Blvd #103 Valley Village, CA 91607
818 980 5999

iBud   7226 Lankershim Blvd North Hollywood, CA 91605
818 255 2211

Illuminati Hollywood   5642 Hollywood Blvd Los Angeles, CA
90028   323 963 4201

Kenmore Medical 261 S Kenmore St Los Angeles, CA 90004
213 384 3881

Kings Palace House   4718 Fountain Ave Unit F Los Angeles, CA
90029   323 660 2665

Korea Town Collective 7382 Melrose Ave Los Angeles, CA 90046
323 951 9513

Kush Stars Hollywood Collective
901 N Western Ave #11 Los Angeles, CA 90029
323 962 3846

Kushmart   6363 Hollywood Blvd Hollywood, CA 90028

LA Alternative Care   7452 Melrose Ave Los Angeles, CA 90046
323 782 1800

La Brea Compassionate Caregivers
735 N La Brea Ave Los Angeles, CA 90038
323 933 4372

LA Buds   5957 Vineland Ave North Hollywood, CA 91601
818 304 2113

LA Compassionate5611 Hollywood Blvd Hollywood, CA 90028

323 460 2113

La Luna 7406 Melrose Ave Los Angeles, CA 90046

323 655 2000

LA Platinum Collective   11554 Vanowen St North Hollywood, CA 91605   818 438 5293

LA Speed Weed   Delivery   888 860 8472

Lankershim Discounts   7401 Lankershim Blvd North Hollywood, CA 91605 818 495 8181

Los Angeles Patients And Caregivers

7213 Santa Monica Blvd West Hollywood, CA 90046

323 882 6033

Mary Janes   4901 Melrose Ave Los Angeles, CA 90029

323 466 6636

MCS   7422 Laurel Canyon Blvd North Hollywood, CA 91605

747 444 8888

Medical Express Delivery Service

Delivery   323 363 8321

MWC   5142 Vineland Ave North Hollywood, CA 91601

818 487 3737

Natural Life Healing   1913 Hyperion Ave Hollywood, CA 90027

323 953 1913

Natural Remedies Caregivers 927 ½ Western Ave Los Angeles, CA 90029   323 871 9500

NoHo 5656   5656 Cahuenga Blvd North Hollywood, CA 91601

818 762 8962

NoHo Gardens House   5627 Lankershim Blvd North Hollywood, CA 91601 818 505 3858

NoHo Organic   11513 Burbank Blvd North Hollywood, CA 91601   818 508 6088

Nug World   4911 Melrose Ave Hollywood, CA 90029

323 463 3920

One Local Green   432 S San Vicente Blvd #100 West Hollywood, CA 90048 855 856 2258

Organic Green Healthcare Collective
5511 Virginia Ave Hollywood, CA 90038
323 516 4921

Patients And Caregivers6141 Vineland Ave North Hollywood, CA 91606   818 588 1307

Pure Decision Association Inc
6122 Santa Monica Blvd Los Angeles, CA 90038
419 600 0000

Purple Paradise Medical Delivery
323 366 0729

Savon Buds   5940 Laurel Canyon North Hollywood, CA 91607
818 666 5050

Sky Hye Collective 6034 Vineland Ave North Hollywood, CA 91606
818 813 7084

Spring Mountain   Delivery   323 540 2971

St Andrews Relief 980 North La Ceinega #102 Los Angeles, CA 90069   424 279 9497

Starlight Wellness Center   1901 Hyperion Ave Hollywood, CA 90027   323 545 2200

Sunny Weed Delivery   626 657 8669

Sunset Green Garden   6013 W Sunset Blvd Hollywood, CA 90028
323 463 6013

The 710 Club   874 N Virgil Ave Hollywood, CA 90029
323 870 7107

The Clinik Caregivers   7133 W Sunset Blvd Los Angeles, CA 90046   323 798 5243

The Connection   Delivery   888 576 3430

The Funhouse   1621 Vista Del Mar Ave Los Angeles, CA 90028
323 905 4386

The Good Life   4316 Melrose Ave Hollywood, CA 90029
    323 407 6015
The Green Easy   7948 West 3rd St Los Angeles, CA 90048
    323 782 0255
The Honey Spot   6775 Santa Monica Blvd Hollywood, CA 90038
    323 819 8036
The NoHo Shop Delivery   Delivery
    818 509 7581
Vapors 13432 Sherman Way North Hollywood, CA 91605
    818 765 2500
VFL Collective   10859 Burbank Blvd Ste A North Hollywood, CA
91601   818 691 3270
    WC   7442 Lankershim Blvd North Hollywood, CA 91605
    818 643 2033
Weedex Collective Delivery   818 308 0768
West Hollywood Healing   8464 Santa Monica Blvd Los
Angeles, CA 90069   323 656 6666
Western Med 938 N Western Ave Los Angeles, CA 90029
    323 798 4246
Western Medical Caregivers   901 N Western Ave #2 Hollywood,
CA 90029 323 455 3848
Wild West Collective   5617 Lakershim Blvd North Hollywood,
CA 91601 818 508 2423
Woodman Canyon Genetics   Delivery
    310 435 0613
World Works Club 6417 Selma Ave Unit B Los Angeles, CA 90028
    323 463 4809
Zen   4702 Vineland Ave North Hollywood, CA 91602
    424 666 9990

San Fernando Valley Area

420 MediCenter 22725 Ventura Blvd Woodland Hills, CA 91364
747 444 9048

6644 Van Nuys Collective 6644 Van Nuys Blvd Van Nuys, CA
91405 818 376 4042

911 Caregivers 9911 Sepulveda Blvd Mission Hills, CA 91345
818 892 9337

AAA Caregivers 12737 Glenoaks Blvd Sylmar, CA 91342
818 403 6164

AAE Medical Care 21612 Roscoe Blvd Canoga Park, CA 91304
818 606 6169

Alternative Medicine Group 10964 Ventura Blvd Studio City, CA
91604 818 762 5886

Apothecary 15372 Dickens St Sherman Oaks, CA 91403
818 905 0420

Ashmoon Caregivers 21777 Ventura Blvd Ste 262 Woodland
Hills, CA 91364 818 716 6200

ATC Lounge 6473 Van Nuys Blvd Van Nuys, CA 91401
818 909 2277

Balboa Med Center 16850 Sherman Way Van Nuys, CA 91406
818 646 0114

Big Mamas Delivery 18446 Hart St Unit M2 Northridge, CA
91324 818 746 7313

Blue Iguana Organics Delivery
818 851 4488

Blue Planet 7301 Sepulveda Blvd Ste 2 Van Nuys, CA 91405
818 782 3949

BLVD Vapors 4463 Van Nuys Blvd Sherman Oaks, CA 91403
818 788 1662

Boo Ku 6817 Sepulveda 2nd Floor Van Nuys, CA 91405
818 908 9255

Buds And Roses Collective 13235 Ventura Blvd Studio City, CA

91604   818 907 8852

Cali Care   Delivery   661 219 3672

Cancare   7570 Winnetka Avenue Winnetka, CA 91306
818 527 1715

Cannalex   13249 Gladstone Ave Sylmar, CA 91342
818 698 4352

Caregivers Express   Delivery
424 266 0029

Caviar Gold Express   Delivery
818 404 2987

CCM Organics   7131 Lindley Ave Reseda, CA 91335
818 708 1700

City Buds   12125 Riverside Dr Studio City, CA 91604
818 281 9627

Cloneville   11422 ½ Moorpark St Studio City, CA 91604
818 627 6874

Compassionate Patient Resource
19237 ½ Ventura Blvd Tarzana, CA 91356
818 996 4277

Cooperative Patients Alliance 4344 Laurel Canyon Blvd Studio City, CA 91604 818 762 7777

CPC   7246 Eton Ave Unit D Canoga Park, CA 91303
818 274 7693

CPPG   7329 Canoga Ave Canoga Park, CA 91367
818 251 9777

Da Vinci   7650 Sepulveda Blvd Van Nuys, CA 91405
747 400 7778

DC Collective   21315 Saticoy St Unit R Canoga Park, CA 91304   818 887 0980

Delta 9 Collective 7648 Van Nuys Blvd Van Nuys, CA 91405
818 997 1003

Down To Earth   23035 Ventura Blvd Ste 101 Woodland Hills, CA 91364 818 222 7395

Emerald Triangle Collective   4638 Tilden Ave Sherman Oaks, CA 91403   323 761 0223

Eve's Garden Collective 5963 Van Nuys Blvd Unit A Van Nuys, CA 91401   818 779 7733

Focus Relief 8247 ½ Sepulveda Blvd Van Nuys, CA 91402   818 891 1010

G Spot Patient Collective   8314 Sepulveda Blvd #B North Hills, CA 91343 818 810 0111

GMCM   18350 Ventura Blvd Tarzana, CA 91356   818 345 1550

Going Green 6309 Van Nuys Blvd Ste 211 Van Nuys, CA 91401   818 689 3328

Green Berrys 13324 Burbank Blvd Sherman Oaks, CA 91401   818 268 5495

Green Cross Collective 6741 Van Nuys Unit B Van Nuys, CA 91405   818 666 9985

Green Cross Wellness   22323 Sherman Way Unit 6 Canoga Park, CA 91303 818 602 0305

Green Dragon Caregivers Inc 7236 Varna Ave North Hollywood, CA 91605 818 442 0054

Green Earth Farmacle   6811 Woodman Ave Van Nuys, CA 91405   818 994 1045

Green Light Delivery   Delivery   424 888 4204

Green Magic 13274 Van Nuys Blvd Suite D Pacoima, CA 91331   818 453 5375

Green Options   16435 Vanowen St Van Nuys, CA 91406   747 888 6623

Green Pearl   13173 Van Nuys Blvd Pacoima, CA 91331

818 899 5544

Green Pearl Delivery   Delivery

661 666 2468

Green St Care Center   12500 Riverside Dr Suite 100 Studio City, CA 91607 818 980 4420

Green Valley Delivery   Delivery

818 675 1070

GreenLeaf Healing Center   14840 Burbank Blvd Sherman Oaks, CA 91411 818 510 0044

Greenlight Discount Pharmacy

15507 Cobalt St #4 Sylmar, CA 91342

818 256 1964

Hai Collective   21001 Sherman Way Ste 12 Canoga Park, CA 91303   818 703 1190

Hazel   17523 Ventura Blvd Encino, CA 91316

818 793 3972

Healters Of Panorama   8205 Woodman St Suite 106 Panorama City, CA 91402 818 849 6688

Heavenly Herbal Collective   7123 Sepulveda Blvd Van Nuys, CA 91405   818 453 8085

Herb Alert   6314 Sepulveda Blvd Van Nuys, CA 91411

818 666 7770

Herbal Healing Solutions   11640 Ventura Blvd Studio City, CA 91604   818 508 7883

Herbal Medicine For You   7035 Reseda Blvd Reseda, CA 91335

818 578 8189

Herbal Solutions Collective   19654 Ventura Blvd Tarzana, CA 91356   818 578 8425

HIP Collective   22831 Ventura Blvd Woodland Hills, CA 91364

818 436 2243

HMC   7207 Balboa Blvd Van Nuys, CA 91406

818 437 8463

Holly Haze Collective   7620 Tampa Ave Reseda, CA 91335
    818 705 4446

House Of Clones   7826 Balboa Blvd Van Nuys, CA 91406
    818 988 9907

Hoyland House   13521 Sherman Way Unit D Van Nuys, CA
91405   818 994 0600

Instagram   Delivery   818 570 4331

Kester   6819 ½ Kester Ave Van Nuys, CA 91405
    818 945 1135

King Meds   14215 Oxnard Blvd Van Nuys, CA 91401
    818 397 3465

Kushism   7555 Woodley Ave Van Nuys, CA 91406
    818 994 3446

MCBP   Delivery   661 904 1894

Medical Herbs 4 U 7122 Reseda Blvd #207 Reseda, CA 91335
    818 666 8080

Meds 215   14530 Arminta St Van Nuys, CA 91402
    818 780 5874

Mega Go   12800 Van Nuys Blvd Suite 4 Pacoima, CA 91331
    747 444 7755

Mendocino Meds   21502 Sherman Way Canoga Park, CA 91303
    818 340 0003

Mission Hills Holistic Remedies
    15534 Devonshire St Unit 104 Mission Hills, CA 91345
    818 893 9091

Mission Hills Organic   10736 Sepulveda Blvd Mission Hills, CA
91345   818 639 6027

MJF Providers   6629 Van Nuys Blvd Ste A Van Nuys, CA 91405
    818 781 0003

MMRC   14303 Ventura Blvd Sherman Oaks, CA 91423

818 783 3888

Mother Natures Remedy   17302 Saticoy St Van Nuys, CA 91406   818 345 MEDS

Mrs Greens Organic Delivery Delivery

818 384 4628

My Buds   14052 Burbank Blvd Sherman Oaks, CA 91401

818 453 8804

Nature's Therapy 19737 Ventura Blvd #205 Woodland Hills, CA 91364   747 477 4707

NCC   7137 Balboa Blvd Van Nuys, CA 91406

747 400 7007

New Age CCC   19720 Ventura Blvd Ste 101 Woodland Hills, CA 91364 818 610 8019

Northridge Caregivers   20465 Sherman Way Canoga Park, CA 91306   818 835 9483

OMG Group 13567 Glenoaks Blvd Sylmar, CA 91342

818 833 9333

On Deck Coop   Delivery   661 474 4632

Open HIP   15242 Parthenia St North Hills, CA 91343

818 894 6965

Organic Health Center 13654 Victory Blvd Van Nuys, CA 91401

818 386 8327

OSH   14064 Foothill Blvd Sylmar, CA 91342

818 454 3976

Ozzys Caregivers 14072 Osbourne St Panorama City, CA 91402

818 830 0320

Panorama Providers   13807 Roscoe Blvd Panorama City, CA 91402   818 894 3300

Perennial Holistic Wellness Center

11705 Ventura Blvd Studio City, CA 91604

818 505 3631

PHC   13131 Van Nuys Blvd Pacoima, CA 91331
818 899 6108

Progressive Options   9901 San Fernando Rd #41 Los Angeles,
CA 91331 818 899 4540

Puffin's Woodland Hills 23002 Ventura Blvd Woodland Hills, CA
91364   818 222 PUFF

Red Moon   14350 Oxnard St Van Nuys, CA 91401
818 997 6912

Remedy 35   17757 Saticoy St Reseda, CA 91335
818 660 2191

Resedas Finest   18340 Sherman Way Reseda, CA 91335
818 708 3994

Resedas Meds   6951 Reseda Blvd Reseda, CA 91335
818 344 3666

Sacred Herb Collective Delivery
Delivery   888 430 3999

San Fernando Valley Patients Group
8244 De Soto Ave Canoga Park, CA 91304
818 727 0420

SCC   13201 Ventura Blvd Studio City, CA 91604
818 386 8500

SFVDM 15223 Burbank Blvd Van Nuys, CA 91411
818 908 9951

SHC   13509 Hubbard St Sylmar, CA 91342
818 384 2522

Sherman Oaks Collective Care
14200 Ventura Blvd #101 Sherman Oaks, CA 91423
818 783 8332

Sherman Oaks Group Collective
15445 Ventura Blvd #1 Sherman Oaks, CA 91403
818 981 1035

Sherman Oaks Holistic Oasis 13650 Burbank Blvd Sherman Oaks, CA 91401 818 997 1787

So Cal Co-op   19459 Ventura Blvd Tarzana, CA 91356
818 344 7622

Spot   10352 Laurel Canyon Blvd Pacoima, CA 91331
818 896 8730

Studio Pharms   12427 Ventura Blvd Studio City, CA 91604
818 980 2100

Sylmar Wellness   12777 San Fernando Rd Unit 10 Sylmar, CA 91342   747 800 7799

Tarzana Herbal Alternative   18816 Ventura Blvd Tarzana, CA 91356   818 609 9666

TeleGram   Delivery   661 349 9028

TFJ   13120 Van Nuys Blvd Unit E Pacoima, CA 91331
818 899 7300

The Best Collective   16031 Sherman Way Van Nuys, CA 91406
818 370 6677

The Flower Shoppe   6742 Van Nuys Blvd #100 Van Nuys, CA 91405   818 582 3794

The Healing Touch   18013 Ventura Blvd Unit A Encino, CA 91316   818 881 1462

The Higher Path   14080 Ventura Blvd Sherman Oaks, CA 91423
818 385 1224

The Hills Collective   20000 Ventura Blvd Woodland Hills, CA 91364   818 835 9596

The Loft   21146 Ventura Blvd Woodland Hills, CA 91364
818 884 LOFT

The Root Cellar   14517 Ventura Blvd Sherman Oaks, CA 91403
818 907 1112

The Verde Vida   Delivery   818 428 5759

Universal Caregivers Inc   13611 Sherman Way Van Nuys, CA

91405   818 988 9333

Valley Green 13703 Burbank Blvd Van Nuys, CA 91401
818 786 8885

Valley Village Delivery   Delivery
818 554 2100

Van Nuys Patient Care   14526 Sherman Way #C Van Nuys, CA 91405   818 916 6012

Van Nuys Wellness Center   6710 Van Nuys Blvd Van Nuys, CA 91405   818 786 0306

VNAS   14434 Gilmore St Van Nuys, CA 91401
818 799 6454

VNHC   15333 Sherman Way Unit G Van Nuys, CA 91406
818 786 2707

VPC   7232 Van Nuys Blvd Ste 103 Van Nuys, CA 91405
818 785 CARE

Wellness Caregivers   6318 Van Nuys Blvd Van Nuys, CA 91401
818 639 2223

Wellness Earth Energy   12021 ½ Ventura Blvd Studio City, CA 91604   818 980 2266

Woodland Hills Treatment Center
5338 Alhama Dr 2nd Floor Woodland Hills, CA 91364
818 884 8338

Your Tree Providers   11048 Ventura Blvd Studio City, CA 91604   818 748 6441

Anaheim Area

1313 Collective Delivery   Delivery
714 820 0522

A City Delivery   Delivery   714 343 1771

A Shelf Above The Rest Delivery
714 512 4081

AHOG Delivery   Delivery   714 818 4882

AMC   306 N State College Blvd Anaheim, CA 92805
    714 597 5424

Anaheim Daily Deals   2173 W Lincoln Anaheim, CA 92801
    714 905 3250

Anaheim Healing Center   126 N Brookhurst St Anaheim, CA
92801   714 760 3745

Burning Treez   Delivery   714 519 6480

Casa De Dabz   1676 W Lincoln Ave Anaheim, CA 92801

Castor Pollux   Delivery   562 372 1110

CCC Collective   1217 S Anaheim Blvd Anaheim, CA 92805
    714 252 3606

Clone Queen 121 N State College #14 Anaheim, CA 92806
    424 209 7746

Dan K Delivery   Delivery   714 422 9959

Doctor A's Delivery   Delivery
    714 678 7907

Droppin Dreams   Delivery   714 470 9977

ExpressMeds Delivery   714 684 6595

Fire Station   1673 W Broadway Unit 3 Anaheim, CA 92807
    714 443 8395

FTP   2530 W Lincoln Ave Suite A Anaheim, CA 92801
    714 683 4679

FTP   Delivery   714 266 9342

HSD   Delivery   714 882 7212

Kush House Delivery   714 261 5768

Med Care   Delivery   714 859 0196

MedLinkOC Delivery   714 273 4152

MYOCTHC Inc   Delivery   714 864 6995

OC Farmacy 3128 W Lincoln Ave Anaheim, CA 92801
    800 420 6935

OC Hotbox   1834 West Lincoln Ave Unit I Anaheim, CA 92801
   714 495 6792
OCD   Delivery   714 276 3666
OCOG   Delivery   714 485 8059
Quick Canna Delivery   Delivery
   714 728 9763
Rite Greens   Delivery   714 558 7167
Royalty Collective Deliveries Delivery
   714 209 6500
Safe Access GKC   2006 W Lincoln Ave Anaheim, CA 92801
   714 818 8822
SoCal Remedies   Delivery   657 210 0665
Sticky Leaf   Delivery   714 343 5697
Take It EZ   Delivery   714 530 3232
The Canna Delivery   Delivery
   714 429 6045
The Green CourierDelivery   714 296 7180

Santa Ana Area
1st St Collective   3701 W 1st St Santa Ana, CA 92703
   714 860 5112
2AM Discount Center   1815 S Main St Santa Ana, CA 92707
   714 659 7927
Access OC Caregivers   1616 E 4th St Ste #130 Santa Ana, CA
92701   714 972 2000
American Collective   1823 E 17th St #113 Santa Ana, CA
92705   714 599 4064
Clone Queen 2961 W McCarthur Blvd #129 Santa Ana, CA 92704
   424 209 7746
EDC   413 W 17th St Ste 106 Santa Ana, CA 92706
   714 332 9325

Emerald   1820 E Garry Ave #204 Santa Ana, CA 92705
714 659 8238
FTP   1820 E Garry Ave #118 Santa Ana, CA 92705
714 650 5536
FTP   1536 E Warner Ave B Santa Ana, CA 92705
714 721 4362
Greenway Healing Center   3220 W Pendleton Ave Santa Ana,
CA 92704 714 545 4040
Kali Buds   1605 W 1st St Ste B Santa Ana, CA 92703
714 559 2061
OC Wellness 3619 W Pendleton Ave Ste A Santa Ana, CA 92704
714 708 2686
OCPC   1921 Carnegie Ave #3H Santa Ana, CA 92705
949 752 6272
OG And Oz   1605 W 1st St Unit C Santa Ana, CA 92703
714 443 8657
One Love PA 1651 East Edinger Ste 104 Santa Ana, CA 92705
714 798 8277
OneStopOC   1823 E 17th St #125 Santa Ana, CA 92725
714 585 5657
Ridiculousness Greens 1425 N Main St Santa Ana, CA 92701
714 388 9492
Saddleback Organics   1320 East St Andrew Place Ste G Santa
Ana, CA 92705 949 529 1420
South Coast Greenz   502 N Euclid Santa Ana, CA 92703
714 278 2663
The Clinic PA1805 East Garry Ave Ste 130 Santa Ana, CA 92705
949 252 0100
Top Shelf Supply 1601 W 1st St Suite A Santa Ana, CA 92705
714 980 3522
TQC   2550 N Grand Ave Santa Ana, CA 92705

714 499 8423

Wax City OC 1820 E Garry Ave Unit 205 Santa Ana, CA 92705
  714 252 3117

Wax House   230 W Warner Ave Unit 105 Santa Ana, CA 92707
  714 905 2203

Wax N Ogs   716 South Main St Santa Ana, CA 92701
  714 953 0419

Wax R Us   1820 E Garry Ave #117 Santa Ana, CA 92705
  714 650 5164

Orange County

1313 Collective Delivery   Delivery
  714 820 0946

American Collective   Delivery
  714 600 2894

Dan K Delivery   Delivery   714 422 9959

Emerald Care Delivery   Delivery
  714 659 8238

Garden Gateway   Delivery   888 315 4679

Genesis Healing   Delivery   714 699 2555

Green Blossom   Delivery   714 655 5962

Green Delivery   Delivery   714 788 8966

Green Delivery   Delivery   714 788 8966

Happy Dayz Health Solutions Delivery
  949 375 8936

Kush Co   Delivery   855 633 8363

Mr Nice Guy Delivery   949 245 9350

Mystery Machine Delivery   714 587 1791

OC Herbal Care   Delivery   949 306 8636

OCPC   Delivery   949 752 6272

OCTA   Delivery   714 349 2172

OrganaCann Wellness Center Delivery
    714 369 8260
PCH   Delivery   714 801 4437
PSA   Delivery   714 721 4362
Rite Greens   Delivery   714 558 7167
SCQM   Delivery   855 420 2420
Sweet C Delivery   714 365 2573
The Goddess Delivers   Delivery
    855 426 5246
The Wax House   Delivery   855 633 8363

San Diego Area
Always Greener   3045 Rosecrans St Ste 310 San Diego, CA 92110   619 806 6814
Central Wellness Collective   2621 El Cajon Blvd San Diego, CA 92104   619 795 7286
Clone Queen 2044 Garnet Ave San Diego, CA 92109
    424 209 7746
Connoisseurs Club   631 S Santa Fe Ave Vista, CA 92083
    760 518 0125
Dank on Turquoise   841 Turquoise St Ste F2 Pacific Beach, CA 92109   858 886 7895
Garnet Greens   936 Garnet Ave Pacific Beach, CA 92109
    858 225 2399
Grand Cass   1012 Grand Ave Pacific Beach, CA 92109
    858 568 6369
Green Diamond Collective   3715 Mission Blvd Pacific Beach, CA 92109   858 488 4372
Green Street Wellness Center 952 Postal Way Ste 6 Vista, CA 92083   855 215 0420
Green Wellness   913 S Coast Hwy Oceanside, CA 92054

760 231 6556

Green Wellness   3045 Rosecrans St Ste 207 San Diego, CA 92110   619 756 7315

Green Wellness   7041 University Ave San Diego, CA 91942   619 303 3344

High Grade Collective   4535 30th San Diego, CA 92116   619 779 3353

Kindest Meds   3455 Camino Del Rio South San Diego, CA 92108   858 333 8062

Medical Alternatives   952 Postal Way Ste 1 Vista, CA 92083   760 917 3485

MJ Wellness Center   2239 Morena Blvd San Diego, CA 92110   619 272 0716

Nature's Alternative Care   5544 La Jolla Blvd San Diego, CA 92037   858 230 6398

Nature's Leaf Collective PB   4502 Cass St #205 2nd Floor Pacific Beach, CA 92109   858 263 4156

Natures Leaf Collective 2525 S Vista Way Carlsbad, CA 92008   760 730 9433

Natures Leaf Collective 212 Broadway Suite B Chula Vista, CA 91910   619 934 6497

North County Botanical 715 Mercantile Vista, CA 92083   800 613 6508

Organic Roots   2603 University Ave San Diego, CA 92104   619 255 6409

Patient Med Ad SD 2015 Garnet Ave Ste 104B Pacific Beach, CA 92109   858 405 6914

PB 4688 Cass St Pacific Beach, CA 92109   619 372 1559

PB Collective 4970 Cass St Pacific Beach, CA 92109   858 273 9333

Rosecrans Wellness Center   1251 Rosecrans St Point Loma, CA 92106   619 523 2295

SoCal Holistic Health   1150 Garnet Ave San Diego, CA 92109   858 524 4928

The OG Clinic   1900 West Vista Way San Marcos, CA 92083   760 758 4201

The Point   2901 Nimitz Blvd San Diego, CA 92106   619 694 4944

The Shop   1020 Grand Ave San Diego, CA 92109   858 568 6474

Riverside County Area

4Evergreen Collective   2781 Rubidoux Rubidoux, CA 92509   951 534 0041

Cannabliss Cooperative Inc   40 South D St Perris, CA 92570   951 292 8136

Canyon Medical Alliance   19700 Temescal Canyon Road Corona, CA 92881   951 427 5066

CAPS   4050 Airport Center Dr Ste C Palm Springs, CA 92264   760 864 8700

Clone Queen 6377 Riverside Ave Riverside, CA 92506   424 209 7746

Creating A Safe Alternative   240 Iowa Ave Riverside, CA 925070   951 684 3956

Desert Organic   19486 Newhall Rd Palm Springs, CA 92262   760 288 4000

Desert Valley Treatment   576 S Williams Rd Palm Springs, CA 92264   760 383 2774

DTPC   9106 Mission Blvd Riverside, CA 92509   951 332 6301

Dutch House Collective 5348 Mission BLV Riverside, CA 92509

951 823 0660

Green Cloud 24877 Sunnymead Blvd Moreno Valley, CA 92553
951 269 5103

Healing Hands Collective   8838 Limonite Ave Riverside, CA
92509   951 685 6570

Herb Town Collective   2351 University Ave Riverside, CA 92505
951 824 9055

Higher Learning   29616 Nuevo Rd Ste A9 Nuevo, CA 92567
951 928 3900

Inland Alternative 5140 Etiwanda Ave Mira Loma, CA 91752
951 360 1000

Jackpot 5543 Mission Blvd Riverside, CA 92509
951 732 0431

Members Apothecary   3848 S McKinely St Ste A Corona, CA
92879   951 536 3048

Mission Blvd Collective 5556 Mission Blvd Ste #101 Jurupa Valley,
CA 92509 951 782 0082

Natural Solutions 31651 US Hwy 74 Homeland, CA 92548
951 926 6611

New Spirit THC   620 Indian Hill Circle Unit D Perris, CA 92570
951 442 8881

Next Level Caregivers   31271 Hwy 74 Homeland, CA 92548
951 926 0261

Ocean Grown   19508 Day St Perris, CA 92570
951 956 8658

Organic Patient Group 10752 Limonite Ave Mira Loma, CA
91752   951 253 5157

Organic Solutions Of The Desert
4765 E Ramon Rd Palm Springs, CA 92264
760 832 7813

Pain Free Collective   72152 Northshore St Ste G Thousand

Palms, CA 92276   760 343 5220

Perris Patients Care   3110 Indian Ave Unit C Perris, CA 92570
951 238 9714

Platinum Collective   12697 Magnolia Ave Corona, CA 92503
951 340 2445

Premier Patient Care   24443 State Hwy 74 Perris, CA 92570
951 443 1144

PS Organica 400 East Sunny Dunes Rd Palm Springs, CA 92264
760 778 1053

Relaxed Expressions Collective
164 Malbert Rd Unit A1 Perris, CA 92570
951 657 4000

THCPlant.Com   440 S El Cielo Rd Palm Springs, CA 92262
909 547 5268

The Lab Collective 9346 Galena St Ste C Riverside, CA 92509
951 360 5654

The Shop   6334 Mission Blvd Riverside, CA 92509
951 742 7070

Twice Green Wellness Center 38813 Nopales Rd Ste B Palm
Desert, CA 92262   760 345 1786

San Bernardino Area

All Private Reserve 3260 N E St Ste A San Bernardino, CA 92404
909 252 2919

Arrow Resurection Discount Meds
265 E Mill St Ste G San Bernardino, CA 92405
909 567 4357

Cali Medicinal   521 N Mountain Ave Upland, CA 91786
909 297 3595

California Collective For Safe Access
214 East Baseline St San Bernardino, CA 92410

909 562 9792

CAMS   7054 Wamego Trail Bldg 1 Yucca Valley, CA 92284
760 418 5743

Clone Queen 8516 Vineyard Ave #409 Rancho Cucamonga, CA
91730   424 209 7746

Clone Queen 2893 Industrial Rd Victorville, CA 92395
424 209 7746

Compassionate Mountain Collective
601 W Big Bear Blvd Big Bear City, CA 92314
909 273 4120

County Line Organics   100 San Bernardino Rd Ridgecrest, CA
93555   760 499 4472

EWC   316 Lankershim Ave Highland, CA 92346
909 749 0533

Green Organic   2085 W Foothill Blvd Upland, CA 91786
909 912 0314

H Street Patient Care   221 H Street Needles, CA 92363
760 326 2455

Higher Healing Medical Center
16209 Main St Hesperia, CA 92345
760 995 4261

HQC   3693 E Highland Ave Ste C Highland, CA 92346
909 547 5167

Jah Healing Caregivers 304 W Big Bear Blvd Big Bear City, CA
92314   909 281 4424

MJ Inc   1092 N E St San Bernardino, CA 92410
951 801 1411

Mojave Desert Wellness Co-Op
1900 Needles Hwy Needles, CA 92363
760 524 7496

Ontana Planet Green   300 J St Needles, CA 92363

760 326 4440
Peoples First 2380 N Garey Ave Pomona, CA 91767
909 753 5810
Positive Health Care   16106 Ceres Ave Ste 107 Fontana, CA
92335   909 749 3504
San Bernardino Collective   1856 Mentone Blvd Ste B Mentone,
CA 92359 909 794 1582
SBPC Shop   154 South E Street San Bernardino, CA 92410
909 203 2670
The 420 Lounge   1179 N E St San Bernardino, CA 92405
909 889 4989
The Dug Out 18319 Valley Blvd Bloomington, CA 92316
909 258 3150
TriCity Patient Center   2174 Foothill Blvd Ste A Upland, CA
91786   909 946 6200
West Coast Alternative 310 W Highland Ave San Barnardino, CA
92405   909 474 9009

Bay Area
7 Star Holistic Healing Center
3288 Pierce St Ste M108 Richmond, CA 94804
510 527 7827
7 Star Meds Dispensary 3823 San Pablo Dam Rd El Sobrante, CA
94803   510 758 6337
Barbary Coast   952 Mission St San Francisco, CA 94103
415 243 4400
Bay Area Safe Alternatives Inc
1326 Grove St San Francisco, CA 94117
415 409 1002
Berkeley Patients Care Collective
2590 Telegraph Ave Berkeley, CA 94704

510 540 7878

Berkeley Patients Group 2366 San Pablo Ave Berkeley, CA 94702
510 540 6013

Bernal Heights Cooperative   33 29th St San Francisco, CA 94110
415 642 5895

Bloom Room 471 Jessie St San Francisco, CA 94103
415 543 7666

Blum Oakland   578 W Grand Ave Oakland, CA 94612
510 338 3632

CBCB   3033 Shattuck Ave Berkeley, CA 94705
510 849 4201

Forty Acres MMGC 1828 San Pablo Ave Berkeley, CA 94702
510 845 4040

Granddaddypurp Collective   2924 Hilltop Mall Road Richmond,
CA 94806 510 243 7575

Grass Roots Clinic 1077 Post St San Francisco, CA 94117
415 346 4338

Green Door   843 Howard St San Francisco, CA 94103
415 541 9590

Green Remedy   2928 Unit C Hilltop Mall Rd Richmond, CA
94806   510 758 7898

Harborside Health Center   1840 Embarcadero Oakland, CA
94606   888 994 2726

Holistic Healing Collective   15501 San Pablo Ave Richmond, CA
94806   510 275 3365

Igzactly 420 527 Howard St San Francisco, CA 94105
415 834 5225

Magnolia Wellness 161 Adeline St Oakland, CA 94607
510 333 6460

Marin Holistic Solutions 200 Tamal Plaza Ste 135 Corte Madera,
CA 94925 415 945 9416

Mission Organic   5258 Mission St San Francisco, CA 94112
   415 585 6337
Oakland Organics 705 Broadway Oakland, CA 94607
   510 444 9420
Ocean Collective   1944 Ocean Ave San Francisco, CA 94127
   415 239 4766
Purple Star MD   2520 Mission St San Francisco, CA 94110
   415 550 1515
Second St Dispensary   70 Second St San Francisco, CA 94105
   415 590 2155
SFFOGG211 12th St San Francisco, CA 94103
   415 896 4271
Shambhala Healing Center   2441 Mission St San Francisco, CA
94110   415 970 9333
  SPARC SF   1256 Mission St San Francisco, CA 94103
   415 252 7727
The Apothecarium2095 Market St San Francisco, CA 94114
   415 500 2620
The Garden Of Eden   21227 Foothill Blvd Castro Valley, CA
94541   510 200 9555
The Good Fellows Smoke Shop
   473 Haight St San Francisco, CA 94117
   415 255 1323
The Love Shack   502 14th St San Francisco, CA 94103
   415 552 5121
TreeMed   5234 Mission St San Francisco, CA 94112
   415 333 7000
Waterfal Wellness 1545 Ocean Ave San Francisco, CA 94112
   415 859 5761
We Are Hemp   913 East Lewelling Blvd Hayward, CA 94541
   510 276 2628

San Jose Area

A2C2 Campbell   3131 S Bascom Ave Ste 220 Campbell, CA 95008   408 429 8405

Amsterdams Garden   2142 The Alameda San Jose, CA 95126   408 717 3035

Bay Leaf   3894 Monterey Hwy San Jose, CA 95111   408 940 4420

Bay Leaf   1692 Tully Rd #3 San Jose, CA 95122   408 532 1933

Buddy's Cannabis Patient Collective   4140 Stevens Creek Blvd San Jose, CA 95129   650 318 3437

CAL MED   973 Park Ave San Jose, CA 95126   408 703 6383

Canna Culture Collective   3591 Charter Park Dr San Jose, CA 95136   408 264 7877

Capitol Collective 459 S Capitol Ave Ste 11 San Jose, CA 95127   408 923 5162

D4L   156 S Jackson Ave San Jose, CA 95116   408 258 8828

Delta Health Center   3114 Story Rd San Jose, CA 95127   408 493 5928

Elemental Wellness   711 Charcot Ave San Jose, CA 95131   408 433 3344

Elixir Medicinal Cannabis Collective   2417 Stevens Creek Blvd San Jose, CA 95128   408 217 8955

Fortune Wellness Center   2231A Fortune Dr San Jose, CA 95131   408 432 1780

Green Jean's Place 3229 South Bascom Ave San Jose, CA 95128

408 429 8506

GSCC   623 N First St San Jose, CA 95112

408 905 0040

Harborside   2106 Ringwood Ave San Jose, CA 95131

888 994 2726

Haze   1814 Hillsdale Ave Ste A San Jose, CA 95124

408 266 HAZE

Herb's 1420 South Winchester Blvd San Jose, CA 95128

408 379 3331

Herb's 282 San Jose Ave San Jose, CA 95125

408 975 9333

Herb's 1641 West San Carlos St San Jose, CA 95128

408 535 6994

Holistic Health Care Cooperative

88 Tully Rd #107 San Jose, CA 95111

408 294 6973

I And I Collective 1530 Alum Rock Ave San Jose, CA 95116

408 649 6925

I And I Collective 2630 Union Ave San Jose, CA 95124

408 879 9187

iMeds   396 South Bascom Ave San Jose, CA 95131

408 642 1367

La Vie   945 S Bascom Ave Unit B San Jose, CA 95128

408 289 1329

Leaf Lab   847 Commercial St San Jose, CA 95112

408 634 5323

Magic Health 1999 Monterey Hwy Ste 100 San Jose, CA 95112

408 291 0080

MedMar   170 S Autumn St San Jose, CA 95110

408 385 9600

MINT   2322 Senter Rd San Jose, CA 95112

408 444 6468

Natural Herbal Pain Relief   519 Parrott St San Jose, CA 95112
408 283 9333

NC3   2175 Stone Ave #1 San Jose, CA 95125
408 490 4805

Nirvana Wellness Center   1926 O'Toole Ave San Jose, CA
95131   408 954 9888

NorCal Care 25 North 14th St Ste 60 San Jose, CA 95112
408 294 6532

Palliative   1670 Zanker Rd Unit A San Jose, CA 95112
408 437 1420

Papadon's Collective   590 Lincoln Ave San Jose, CA 95126
855 PAPADON

Papadon's Collective   931 Commercial St San Jose, CA 95112
408 392 8260

Patient 2 Patient 1692 Tully Rd #6 San Jose, CA 95122
408 238 4800

Peace Of Mind   471 Willow St San Jose, CA 95125
408 293 2179

Platinum Society 1174 Lincoln Ave San Jose, CA 95125
408 466 8468

Purple Lotus Patient Center   903 Commercial St Ste 50 San Jose,
CA 95112 408 456 0420

Pyramid Medicinal Dispensary
90 E Gish Rd #250 2nd Floor San Jose, CA 95112
408 657 6753

Revolution Health 1621 Almaden Rd San Jose, CA 95125
408 289 1694

San Jose Medicinal 52 South First St Suite 220 San Jose, CA 95113
408 275 0384

San Jose Organics 88 Tully Rd #100 San Jose, CA 95111

408 977 0420

San Jose Sanative Solutions Center

   581 E Taylor St San Jose, CA 95112

   408 418 3352

Santa Cruz Naturally   93 N 14th St San Jose, CA 95112

   408 416 3398

Serenity Collective 2601 Senter Rd San Jose, CA 95111

   408 781 4516

Silicon Valley ARC 246 East Gish Rd San Jose, CA 95112

   408 642 1089

Simply Chronic Healing 970 Story Rd San Jose, CA 95122

   408 462 5673

SJ Patients Group 824 The Alameda San Jose, CA 95126

   408 295 5411

South Bay CRC   90 Great Oaks Blvd Ste 202 San Jose, CA 95119

   408 224 6000

South Bay Healing Center   991 Saratoga Ave Ste 140 San Jose, CA 95129 408 899 4676

South Bay Natural Remedies Dispensary

   2950 Daylight Way San Jose, CA 95111

   408 226 7000

South Valley Rx   5591 Snell Ave San Jose, CA 95123

   408 360 0503

Story Wellness   1221 Story Rd Ste 40 San Jose, CA 95122

   408 295 0888

SVCare 1711 Hamilton Ave Ste B San Jose, CA 95125

   408 264 4200

SVCare 2591 S Bascom Ave Unit 1 San Jose, CA 95008

   408 559 4200

The All American Cannabis Club

   1082 Stockton Ave San Jose, CA 95110

408 293 0420

The Portal Herbal Health Collective
1141 Ringwood Ct Ste 100 San Jose, CA 95131
408 526 0420

Yerba Buena 1324 N 10th St San Jose, CA 95112
888 539 8470

Yerba Buena 4211 Barrymore Dr San Jose, CA 95117
888 539 8470

Yerba Buena 2129 S 10th St San Jose, CA 95112
888 539 8470

Yerba Buena 4464 Pearl Ave San Jose, CA 95136
888 539 8470

Yerba Buena 325 S Monroe St San Jose, CA 95128
888 539 8470

Bakersfield Area

AGF   521 H St Bakersfield, CA 93304
661 873 4788

AMG   1820 Brundage Lane Ste C Bakersfield, CA 93304
661 843 7757

Casa BMC   907 34th St Bakersfield, CA 93301
661 331 4522

Clone Queen 1200 21st St Bakersfield, CA 93301
424 209 7746

Collectively Grown Inc   1410 Wible Rd #103 Bakersfield, CA
93304   661 847 9779

Garden Of Bliss Inc   1131 Niles St #C Bakersfield, CA 93305
661 327 4480

Golden State Cooperative   1703 27th St Bakersfield, CA 93301
661 321 0900

Green Cross 707 ½ Niles St Bakersfield, CA 93305

661 869 0211

Green Earth Remedies   2421 Haley St #11 Bakersfield, CA 93305
661 872 6420

Green Remedies III   1801 Hasti Acers Ste 3 Bakersfield, CA 93309   661 831 6420

HH   131 Chester Ave #B Bakersfield, CA 93301
661 322 5874

Highway 99 Collective   19456 Columbo St Ste H Bakersfield, CA 93308   661 281 7678

HLC Collective   407 18th St Bakersfield, CA 93301
661 432 7070

Leaf   210 Monterey St Bakersfield, CA 93305
661 322 7777

Nature's Medicinal 2816 K St Bakersfield, CA 93301
661 325 0210

ODC   107 17th St Bakersfield, CA 93301
661 631 1390

Safe Collective   2850 S Chester Ave Ste B Bakersfield, CA 93304   661 831 7002

Taft Hwy Collective   3024 Taft Hwy Bakersfield, CA 93313
661 381 7570

V And G Collective 2309 Chester Ave Bakersfield, CA 93301
661 327 9000

Sacramento Area

A Therapeutic Alternative   3015 H St Sacramento, CA 95816
916 822 4717

Abatin Wellness Center 2100 29th St Sacramento, CA 95817
916 822 5699

All Natural Inc   4151 South Shingle Rd #2 Shingle Springs, CA 95682   530 676 4032

Alpine Alternative 8112 Alpine Ave Sacramento, CA 95826
916 739 6337

CC101 6435 Florin Perkins Rd Sacramento, CA 95828
916 387 6233

Cloud 95711 Florin Perkins Rd #A Sacramento, CA 95828
916 387 8605

Foothill Health And Wellness 3830 Dividend Dr Ste A Shingle
Springs, CA 95682   530 676 4532

Horizon Collective 3600 Power Inn Rd Sacramento, CA 95826
916 455 1931

Hugs Alternative Care   2035 Stockton Blvd Sacramento, CA
95817   916 452 3699

MIA   1404 28th St Sacramento, CA 95816
916 451 3081

MMCA   3031 Alhambra Dr Ste 102 Cameron Park, CA 95682
530 677 5362

Nor Cal Alternative Healing   515 Broadway Sacramento, CA
95818   916 519 8899

Nor Cal Extracts   316 J St Sacramento, CA 95618
916 623 5473

Northstar Holistic Collective 1236 C St Sacramento, CA 95814
916 476 4344

Pure Life Collective   537 Pleasant Valley Rd #2 Diamond
Springs, CA 95619   530 622 7873

RCP   1508 El Camino Ave Sacramento, CA 95815
916 925 5696

Safe Capitol Compassion Coop
135 Main Ave Sacramento, CA 95838
916 254 3287

Two Rivers   315 North 10th St Sacramento, CA 95811
916 804 8975

Valley Health Options   1421 Auburn Blvd Sacramento, CA 95815
916 779 0715

Central California Area
All Green Collective   2753 Diamond St Rosamond, CA 93560
661 256 6493
Antelope Valley Diamond Collective
1733 Sierra Hwy Rosamond, CA 93560
661 256 7753
Blue Mountain Collective   692 Marshall Ave Ste A San Andreas,
CA 95249 209 754 3289
Calaveras Medical Collective 1919 Vista Del Lago St #6 Valley
Springs, CA 95252   209 920 3634
California Growers Collective 3711 A Soquel Dr Soquel, CA 95073
831 600 7744
Cannacanhelp Inc 6614 Ave 304 Goshen, CA 93291
559 651 4090
Capitola Healing Association Inc
3088 Winkle Ave Ste C Santa Cruz, CA 95065
831 475 5506
Central Coast Wellness Center
6235 Hwy 9 Felton, CA 95018
831 704 7340
Clone Queen 1841 W Ave Ste K1 Lancaster, CA 93534
424 209 7746
Collective 1950   1950 W Freemont St Stockton, CA 95203
209 808 5616
Creekside Collective   13266 Hwy 9 Boulder Creek, CA 95006
831 338 3840
Evolution   6116 Hwy 9 Unit #1 Felton, CA 95018
831 704 7151

Granny Purps   2649 41st Ave Soquel, CA 95073
831 477 7500

Gray Sky Alternative Medicine
9150B E Lacey Blvd Hanford, CA 93230
559 410 3076

Green Acres 3912 Portola Dr Ste 1 Santa Cruz, CA 95062
831 475 8420

Green Mammoth   94 Laurel Mt Rd Ste 420 Mammoth Lakes, CA 93546   760 934 5400

Greenway Compassionate Relief
140 Dubois St #D Santa Cruz, CA 95073
831 420 1640

Herbal Cruz Inc   1001 41st Ave Santa Cruz, CA 95062
831 462 9999

Hwy 138 Collective   13120B Pearblossom Hwy Pearblossom, CA 93553 661 944 9140

Kiona's Farmacy   7450 River Road Oakdale, CA 95361
209 602 4732

Kiona's Farmacy   2650 W Byron Rd Tracy, CA 95377
209 914 3382

Little Trees Wellness Collective
2641 Hwy 4 Ste 7A Arnold, CA 95223
209 736 7635

Mammoth Lakes Wellness   3399 Main St Ste Q1 Mammoth Lakes, CA 93546   760 924 2299

Mother Nature Inc 1427 South Lexington St Delano, CA 93215
661 778 0893

Organic Health Solutions   1315 W Rosamond Blvd Ste 1A Rosamond, CA 93560   661 256 0220

Queens Botanica 7606 Pearblossom Hwy Little Rock, CA 93543
661 547 9137

Santa Cruz Mountain Herbs   22990 Hwy 17 Unit C Los Gatos, CA 95033   408 455 1060

Santa Cruz Mountain Naturals
9077 Soquel Dr Aptos, CA 95003
831 688 SCMN

Sticky Icky Delano Co-Op   605 Main St Delano, CA 93215
661 474 5057

Stockton Specialty 1804 Country Club Blvd Stockton, CA 95204
209 469 0534

The Healing Cooperative   4124 Lake Isabella Blvd Lake Isabella, CA 93205   760 379 2474

Therapeutic Healing Center   40713 Hwy 41 Oakhurst 8A Oakhurst, CA 93644 559 676 2783

Therapeutic Healthcare 5011 Soquel Dr Santa Cruz, CA 95073
831 713 5641

Tulare Alternative Health Center
260 N L St Tulare, CA 93274
559 688 4420

Tulare Alternative Relief Association
150 North J St Tulare, CA 93274
559 688 2001

Waterloo Wellness 2370 Waterloo Rd Stockton, CA 95205
209 227 8195

West Coast   3236 N Tracy Blvd Tracy, CA 95376
209 207 9308

Humboldt Area

Collective Conscious Apothecary
13325 South Hwy 101 Hopland Mendocino, CA 95449
707 744 1565

Compassionate Heart   190 Kuki Lane Ukiah, CA 95482

707 462 5100

D And M Compassion Center 14491 Olympic Dr Clearlake, CA 95422   707 994 1320

Herban Legend   17875 N Hwy 1 Fort Bragg, CA 95437
707 961 0113

Humboldt Patient Resource Center
980 6th St Arcata, CA 95521
707 826 7988

Lakeside Herbal Solution   4345 Mullen Ave Clearlake, CA 95422   707 994 3721

Love In It Cooperative   10464 Lansing St Mendocino, CA 95460
707 937 3123

The Humboldt County Collective
1670 Myrtle Ave Ste B Eureka, CA 95501
707 442 2420

The Leonard Moore Co-Op   44970 Ukiah St Mendocino, CA 95460   707 937 4562

Triple C Collective 14196 Lakeshore Dr Clearlake, CA 95422
707 701 4160

Northern California Area

101 North   40 Tennessee St Vallejo, CA 94590
707 980 7937

530 Collective   1550 Locust Ave Shasta Lake City, CA 96019
530 275 0420

Alternatives Health Collective
1603 Hampton Way Santa Rosa, CA 95407
707 525 1420

California Collective Care   707 643 6313
707 643 6313

California Herbal Relief Center

1971 Broadway Vallejo, CA 94589
707 731 2460
Enhanced Energies   1804 Capitol St Vallejo, CA 94590
707 557 5660
Greenleaf Solutions   650 Benicia Rd Vallejo, CA 94591
707 563 8259
Hearts Of Mt Shasta   408 South Mt Shasta Blvd Mt Shasta, CA
96067   530 926 6337
Hwy 29 Health Care   3737 Sonoma Blvd Vallejo, CA 94590
707 645 8303
Mercy Wellness Of Cotati   7950 Redwood Dr Ste 8 Cotati, CA
94931   707 795 1600
Natures Love Collective 308 Tennessee St Vallejo, CA 94590
707 557 2239
OrganiCann 301 East Todd Rd Santa Rosa, CA 95407
707 588 8811
Peace In Medicine 6771 Sebastopol Ave #100 Sebastopol, CA
95472   707 823 4206
Peace In Medicine 1061 North Dutton Ave Santa Rosa, CA 95404
707 843 3227
Redwood Herbal Alliance   5270 Aero Drive Santa Rosa, CA
95403   707 528 3632
ReLeaf Alternative 419 Georgia St Ste #30 Vallejo, CA 94590
707 980 7868
Riverside Wellness Collective 15025 River Rd Guerneville, CA
95446   707 869 8008
Sonoma County Collective   4170 Santa Rosa Ave Santa Rosa, CA
94507   707 542 7420
Tahoe Wellness Cooperative 3445 Lake Tahoe Blvd South Lake
Tahoe, CA 96150   530 544 8000
The Family Tree Care Center 999 Mission De Oro Dr Ste 104

Redding, CA 96003   530 605 3636
   The Florist   850 Redwood St Ste A Vallejo, CA 94590
      707 647 1127
   The Green Heart   625 S Mt Shasta Blvd Mt Shasta, CA 96067
      530 918 9440
   The Queen Of Dragons 5044 Shasta Dam Blvd Shasta Lake City,
CA 96019 530 276 9771
   US Bloom   1201 Springs Rd Vallejo, CA 94590
      707 561 0716
Vallejo Holistic Health Center
      1516 Napa St Vallejo, CA 94590
      707 652 5018